# Unconventionally Successful

Out of the Box Thoughts and Actions that
Led to Extraordinary Outcomes

By Christopher W. Albrecht

NFB Publishing
Buffalo, New York

Copyright © 2020 Christopher W. Albrecht

Printed in the United States of America

UNCONVENTIONALLY SUCCESSFUL: Out of the Box Thoughts and Actions that Led to Extraordinary Outcomes/ Albrecht— 1st Edition

ISBN: 978-0-9978317-7-1

1. Title.
2. Education.
3. Education Philosophy.
4. Interviews.
5. Albrecht.

No part of this book may be reproduced or transmitted in any form by any means, electronic or mechanical, including photocopying, recording, or by any information storage and retrieval system without permission in writing by the author.

Front cover picture taken by Alexandra Covert and edited by Michael LaFrance.

Back cover image courtesy of Dr. Irving Finkel of the British Museum of History.

NFB
NFB Publishing/Amelia Press
119 Dorchester Road
Buffalo, New York 14213

For more information visit Nfbpublishing.com

Grateful acknowledgment from the author is made to Mark Pogodzinski, publisher, and Sarah Page, Caurrie Putnam-Ferguson and Debbie Moyer, editors.

Twitter: @Albrecht_NYSTOY

To my wife,
Jennifer Howard Albrecht

…and a dog named Harley, who warmed my feet while I wrote this book.

## Table of Contents

| | |
|---|---|
| **Foreword and Dedication** | I |
| **Introduction** | XI |
| **Interview with Abby Wambach** | 1 |
| **Chapter 1:** *Common Threads,* | |
| *Core Values & Innovation* | 7 |
| **Interview with Sal Kahn** | 47 |
| **Chapter 2:** *The Toppling Dominos and* | |
| *The Effect of Timing* | 55 |
| **Interview with Nicole Dreiske** | 85 |
| **Chapter 3**: *Glenn Cunningham:* | |
| *The Underestimation of Soft Skills* | 93 |
| **Interview with Homer Hickam** | 119 |
| **Chapter 4:** *Harry Coover,* | |
| *Jack McKissick & Vision Value* | 125 |
| **Interview with Ed Buckbee** | 147 |
| **Chapter 5:** *What Alan Shepard Discovered* | |
| *the Night Before the Launch* | 159 |
| **Interview with Stephen Duckworth** | 181 |
| **Chapter 6:** *Rubber Meets Responsibility* | 193 |

**INTERVIEW WITH JAHANA HAYES**     219
**CHAPTER 7:** *The Curious Circumstances of the
      Jefferson Memorial and Paul Revere*     225

**INTERVIEW WITH RANDALL MCDANIEL**     243
**CHAPTER 8:** *Noah's Boat Was Round: History,
      Its Writers, & Who Really Matters*     251

**CONCLUSION**     275

**EPILOGUE**     279

# Foreword and Dedication

I will warn you right out of the gate, this book is a lot like a racquetball being smacked around the court. It is a little quirky, is loaded like a stuffed potato with interesting tidbits from history, current trends, and research, and has eight amazing interviews with some unique individuals. If you are looking for a book that will make you mentally examine our world through lenses that you may never have considered, I believe you picked up the right one. If you liked connect the dots books as a child, this book will give you that same warm and fuzzy feeling when you finally realize what the big picture is. The following pages are full of "dots" to connect.

Truthfully, when I was seventeen, I thought I was going to be an Air Force pilot. I lived through the Top Gun years and was convinced that all pilots were just like Tom Cruise. I wound up becoming a teacher and have taught for a quarter of a century. How that happened is a story for another book. I have never kept a journal. Maybe I should have. The years I have spent in the classroom have been filled with emotion, passion, laughter, and tears. Many of the stories from my career have faded in my mind over time, but occasionally, something or someone will jog my memory, and I realize how lucky I am. I have spent my career helping children be successful. I challenge anybody to come up with a better job description.

I will never concede to the notion that simultaneously trying to reach twenty-five nine-year-old kids is easy, even if they are clones of one another. What is not stated in the job description of a teacher is that there is no way to conventionally teach because every student is unique. Just when I think I have seen it all or get that kaboom feeling like I did when I solved one side of a Rubik's Cube, something new happens. (I still cannot fully solve the Rubik's Cube.) To help my students fill their mental buckets, I have learned the art of teaching unconventionally.

The art of working unconventionally with children to help them be successful often feels like the first time I tried chopsticks. It takes a lot of practice and patience, and there have been times that I caved in, put down the chopsticks, and grabbed a spoon. If I were to start my career all over again, there is only one thing that I would change: I would have tried to capture each unconventional thing that I have done and experienced. I think a lot of wisdom could have been chronicled from so many unique experiences. However, I do remember the beginning, and that is where I will start.

### New Martinsville, West Virginia
### 1995

I WAS PULLING my hair out crawling around the dusty and dirty ceiling tiles of the school dragging an Ethernet cable. I was fresh out of college and bewildered. A month before I had been looking for an elementary school teaching job, but the only position I was able to land was one teaching half time middle school technology.

To add to the challenge, I was teaching kindergarten in the afternoon. So why was I in a ceiling?

It was 1995, and there was this new cutting-edge technology called the internet that was overrunning schools across the country. I was clueless. I barely knew how to save a file to a floppy disk, and now I was supposed to network computers? I had little money, was recently married, and had no choice but to accept this teaching position.

In desperation, I had telephoned the savior who coached me through high school calculus: my best friend, Jeff. He was fresh out of college too, and I concluded since he was going to work for the National Security Agency in Washington, D.C., he would surely know some top-secret method to unlock this mess. When I called him, he just laughed.

It was hot and stuffy above the ceiling tiles, and I was alone on the third Saturday of the school year. That was when I heard a voice from below. I stuck my head upside down out of the ceiling and recognized another Jeff. This person was not Jeff in Washington; it was Jeff, a 12-year-old student from my second period computer technology class. He had wandered into the school because I had propped the doors open trying to get ventilation. He stared blankly at me and asked, "What are you doing up there?"

Instead of answering his question, I responded, "Do you have any idea what this thing called the internet is?"

"Oh, yeah, that. Sure. I know all about it. Why?"

"Grab the ladder and come up."

That was how I started my career. In the months leading up to

## IV   Unconventionally Successful

my job teaching technology and kindergarten, I imagined my days sitting on a carpet decorated with a picture of the United States, surrounded by twenty third graders. Instead, it started in the dusty ceiling of the middle school wing with Jeff. It was an unconventional start to a career and not what I expected. That first weekend it was just Jeff and me up there in that ceiling. The next weekend three more 'Jeffs' showed up. One Saturday later there were ten Jeffs. How did these kids know how to wire a school? All I knew was that my abilities and knowledge were distant from my goal, and they were closing that gap.

After a year of crawling through dirty ceilings and under undusted tables, an army of Jeffs had three-hundred computers with boosted memory all networked. We had a school webpage (the first in West Virginia), and I won national recognition for being an innovator.

Three years later, I had to leave the Jeffs to seek out that elementary classroom I so desired. My wife and I relocated from West Virginia after the birth of our daughter to where we grew up. I finally got that carpet with a map of the United States on it, though it was in a fourth-grade classroom. What happened to all those Jeffs? From our tiny rural town in West Virginia, many of them became highly successful. One now works at MIT and another for NASA. By metaphorically removing the ceiling of learning off my classroom, I allowed my students to discover a world they may not have found on their own.

My life story, up to this point, has transpired unconventionally. Though I am a teacher, I am also a lifelong learner. Instead of being the traditional imparter of knowledge, I spend my days at school facilitating my students' dreams and educations with gentle guidance. I am unconventional, and it works.

### Brockport, New York, over 20 years later…

AUGUST IS A special month for teachers. Roughly the second week of the month, a letter appears in my mailbox from school. I anticipate it more than the tax return check. The letter is my roster for the upcoming school year. When that envelope arrives, I do not open it gingerly. This moment is like Christmas, and I rip it open quickly. I have grown to recognize that each child in that class will bring along a whole new experience, and only that child can say what the journey is going to be.

A few years ago, I was standing there in my driveway having Christmas in August, examining the names of that year's class. The class roster was different from any other I had ever seen. The first five students on the roster all had the same surname. It was a name I did not recognize, so I guessed that they might be cousins. I called the school. Our secretary informed me that the five students were not cousins but rather quintuplets! Three girls and two boys, all from the same birth, were in my class. I was in disbelief.

Adventures happen in all different ways. What I know is that as a teacher I teach, but equally important is that I learn. I knew nothing about cerebral palsy when the quintuplets arrived. All I knew was that there were three girls and two boys. However, one of the boys was challenged with cerebral palsy. He had many strengths. He was kind, well-liked, and a great hugger. There were several challenges, too. His ability with depth perception and walking were noticeably impacting his capacity to do many things, and I could see his frustration.

A lot of fourth graders become self-aware of their abilities, and this young man was no exception. So, after a discussion with his parents, we decided to teach him about cerebral palsy. No materials were available that were appropriate for him. Therefore, he wrote a book about his own life. In his book, he revealed that his dream was to become a police officer.

How was I going to help this young man achieve his dream? I was stumped. My mind traveled back twenty years to those days of crawling above dusty ceilings wiring a computer network. I was faced with a whirlwind of emotions: fear, concern, and confusion. However, now I was much older, and I understood the positive consequence of having faith in educating unconventionally. I have remained true to living unconventionally, and it was about to serve my student and me well once again.

As a teacher, I recognize that a large part of my mission is to help all children discover and work toward their dreams. I had unlocked what seemed to me an impossible dream. What I discovered in my first weeks of teaching in West Virginia would play a pivotal role here. When this child presented his dream of becoming a police officer, I could not envision it. However, these challenges are where unconventional thinking lives. I felt that the space between his abilities and his dream was too vast, and I did not have any answers about how he could get there. He did.

I am a teacher, but more importantly, I am forever a learner. The truth was that this young man needed to tell me what he would have to do to complete his dream. He just said, "I need to run so I can catch the bad guys." In West Virginia, I accomplished my goals by crawling. This child understood that his dream started with running.

Running seemed simple enough. It was not. We stayed after school to run. My student made it 200 yards. However, he wanted to do it again a few days later. We had the same outcome. Just as I hadn't been a designer of computer networks, I was not a running coach. I needed guidance. I consulted with all the therapists he worked with, and his adaptive physical education teacher explained to me how we could not merely stretch like I usually do before a run. We had to learn cerebral palsy-specific stretches that addressed his stiff joints and muscles. I also believed a team approach would be helpful, so I made an offer to the class to join us, and suddenly we had a team of five. Our ragtag bunch ran at different paces, so we used the track. With some stretching, some pain, remarkable determination, and much work, we were running a mile in five weeks. A mile was a huge accomplishment.

For the first time, my student was beginning to lead, not by distance and speed, but by stretches and example. This young man was becoming our team captain. We were now not only there to help him become a police officer; every team member set their own goals. We ran three times per week, and by late April, we were approaching two miles.

That was when one of our runners suggested that we run a marathon. In the adult world, a marathon is 26.2 miles, but I figured that in a kid's world a 5K would work. With the agreement of all five students and their families, we now had a targeted goal. When we set that goal, no one on the team had ever run three miles. A 5K is just over that at 3.1 miles. Did we have the ability to reach our dreams?

The week before the race, our captain was struggling with swelling and pain. I was assured that he was not damaging himself, and he would not give up. Remember, initially, this was his dream that we were chasing.

The day of the race arrived. On a sunny Saturday in late May we ran, and without stopping, all students and adults finished the 5K. What about my student with cerebral palsy? He never stopped running once, completing the race in 41 minutes. Unexpectedly, along with his success in running, he was now making tremendous growth academically. He was a student who required assistive technology, but now he was writing paragraphs with a pencil and keeping pace with the class.

The following year, we ran again. Without recruiting, our team grew to nineteen. People recognized unconventional success. Our captain was not fearful about finishing the race, and he now was coaching the new runners who had joined us. He knew he had achieved the dream of running a 5K and was serving others by helping them do the same.

In the third year of our team, the young man, now in middle school, ran a 5K race in 35 minutes and 2 seconds, a personal best by over six minutes. That year we allowed the team to grow even more unconventional. A critical characteristic of runners is that they must want to be there. Running is mentally and physically punishing, and therefore, if a person is forced, running becomes misery. In a unique twist, we took away the age limits of the team. Our youngest member was an eight-year-old second grader, and our oldest runner was a 54-year-old man who was battling diabetes. After losing twenty-five pounds, this man had control of his diabetes. This was one of many ripple effects caused by one child having the grit to run.

The next year, we grew to thirty-seven runners, all supporting each other with our individual goals and challenges. We never recruited. In year four, we swelled to forty runners. This team represented precisely what unconventional success is all about.

When my student presented his dream of becoming a police officer, I could not see it as a possibility; I only saw challenges that seemed too great to overcome. I did not have the answers, but he did, and his attitude of *I can do it* moved so many others to say *we can do it*.

I must keep on learning. We all need to commit ourselves to lifelong learning habits in the context of the lives we lead. No two people are alike, and often I need to think unconventionally to help my students find the path to success. This is challenging. Arguably, there are more distractions in today's world that put roadblocks in the way of personal growth. Though only parts of this book discuss the topic of education, the entire book was built on the notion that nearly all of us need some unconventional training. How does running affect academic performance? Just ask that young man who runs despite having cerebral palsy. How does a newly hired teacher who knows nothing about computers in 1995 move an entire school into the internet era? Just ask the students who crawled with me through my first year of teaching.

From its inception, my friend and professional writer, Caurie Putnam-Ferguson, provided me with guidance, insight and inspirational words as I worked on this project. Her encouragement and positive attitude are immeasurable. I owe a debt of gratitude to the two schools I have taught at: New Martinsville School in New Martinsville, West Virginia and the Fred W. Hill School in Brockport, New York. My life has been touched in so many ways by these amazing and magical places. Thank you to my community, the family of students that I have devoted my soul to, and my own family and friends for embracing me for who I am. For all those people who have accepted me for the unconventional teacher, thinker, creator, husband, father, and dreamer that I am, this book is dedicated to you.

> *-Narrative adapted from my 2018 TEDx Talk entitled "Dust and Sneakers, Crawling and Walking."*

# Introduction

> *"For I know the plans I have for you to prosper you and not to harm you, plans to give you hope and a future."*
>
> —*Jeremiah 29:11*

THE DRIVE TO WRITE *Unconventionally Successful* developed from years of teaching in a public school system. I have nearly twenty-five years of service as a public school teacher. I work with children, communities, government standards and policies, administrators, and a diversity of families with their challenges and advantages. In 2017, I was named the 2018 New York State Teacher of the Year, and in 2019, I was inducted into the National Teachers Hall of Fame. These experiences have given me even greater exposure, diverse experiences, and training with teachers, politicians, private citizens, corporations, and groups that expand to a global network. There is a lot more that goes into the driving force of our world than what is explicit and easy to identify. After visiting over seventy-five schools in one year, my notion was confirmed that schools and communities are like fingerprints, each very different from one another. The school visits solidified my understanding that there is a vast world of wonderful stories and pockets of culture that lay disguised behind a curtain of what the media deems newsworthy. I began writing this book in 2016, and those precious times witnessing the untold stories in schools provided me with the final nudge to complete it. *Unconventionally Successful* is designed to help you examine trends in our society and their nearly disguised effect on all people, young and old.

My superintendent of schools understood the unique opportunity of being a Teacher of the Year and advised me to journal the experience. At that point, only 47 other people in the history of New York had received this honor. She explained that I was going to get a glimpse of a world that few get to see. She was right.

I tried journaling, but it just felt like torture. When I was ten, my mom gave me a Snoopy diary for Christmas with a real lock and key; I think it was a way of tricking me into writing more. The "cool factor" of a lock on a book wore off after two entries. I was 45 years old when I became Teacher of the Year. My desire to journal had not improved much, though I am proud to say I journaled seven entries over the first ten days of being a Teacher of the Year. So, from age ten to now, I know that I can write five more entries than I could tolerate as a ten-year-old before completely throwing in the towel.

Teachers live their lives vicariously through the joy of others. In some ways, being a Teacher of the Year is paradoxical. Teaching is a lot like being the assistant coach on a successful team; you must do a great job but let the players (or students) shine. Education is not a profession for glory. Instead, teachers celebrate when success befalls their students. As a Teacher of the Year, I felt very uncomfortable. I was receiving the attention that I was always happy to see my students get.

In January of "the big year," all the Teachers of the Year were flown out to San Francisco, California. It was the first time I got to meet the other fifty-five state Teachers of the Year. One teacher came from every state, as well as from each of the US territories and the Department of Defense. The first meeting felt like a Miss America pageant. Instead of saying my name, I walked around saying, "Yes, I am New York."

Being a Teacher of the Year is a trick. Nobody told me that I was going to be trained morning to night, lead a crazy presentation schedule, and not get paid for any of it. Nobody explained that I would be eating my dinners while driving all over the place. I still had to teach fourth grade by day, but after school hours I had to fulfill the many presentation requests that came with my new title. Everyone ate while I presented. Then, I took what dinner I could find. My car seat is a roadmap of stains from food I ate on the long drives.

Between teaching during the day and presenting at night, my schedule was packed, but there were other tasks that were expected of us. One of the very first tasks we were given was to design a Google doodle. For one day, every person in the world who logged onto Google would see our artwork wrapped around the Google logo. At that point a revelation hit me. I was 3,000 miles away from home working with a person whose sole job was to draw Google doodles! When on Earth would I ever get this opportunity again? So, I pulled out my phone, started the voice recorder and asked Lydia, the thirty-year-old Google doodler, if I could interview her. The only question that came to mind was, "Who is your favorite teacher?" These interviews replaced my journal.

By December of 2018, I had recorded hundreds of interviews. I never changed the question. As I interviewed people, I began to see parallels between the messages that I was writing about in the original format of this book and the recollections I heard in the interviews. After many hours of listening, I decided to pair one conversation with each chapter. Each interview consisted of memories tucked away for decades. Time filters out what really matters in a person's life, and this allows the interviews to shed light on the lifelong impact educators make. It also proved to me that the path of most people's lives follows a similar pattern parallel to the stories I was writing about. Most people have unconventional stories about their time in school.

Before each chapter, I include the exact transcript of a conversation coupled with a reflection of how the story that each person shared sheds light on what matters when it comes to education. What is clear: it is not what you teach, but how you teach that matters. Some of the interviews are hard to read because they are typed from the exact words that were said. I felt it was important to preserve the words because in many cases, the words and mannerisms of each person I interviewed reveal a lot about them.

I consider the work of teachers to be one of the greatest endeavors on the planet. Teachers spend their days helping students become ready for the real world. One goal I set when I first outlined this book was to focus in on stories in which familiar and unfamiliar central figures have positive and negative effects on others. As the title indicates, causes and effects sometimes develop in unconventional ways.

If our goal is to make progress, we need to understand the basis and the root cause for success and failure. The first page of this book was written months before I became a Teacher of the Year. The final edits were made after I became a member of the National Teacher Hall of Fame. After interviewing so many amazing people and hearing such compelling stories about their favorite teachers, I knew I would have to include some interviews with my commentary in this book.

Before a baseball game, most teams take batting practice. Exceptional players are cautious that each swing made during batting practice is precise. Repetition develops muscle memory. If a physical skill is repeated the same way over and over, eventually when that skill is put to the test in a game, the body will do what has been built into its memory. Hitting a baseball is an example of a cerebral act in which the hitter uses muscle memory. *Unconventionally Successful* was written with the intent to provide a wide variety of cases focused on similar patterns. The reader may be challenged to look differently at the underlying circumstances of outcomes with the ability to look at any result and examine it unconventionally.

It brings me great joy that you have chosen to read this book, which I devoted much time too. I hope you enjoy it.

# Interview with Abby Wambach
*November 2, 2018*
*Brooklyn, New York*

*I had the pleasure of meeting Abby Wambach in Brooklyn, New York while sitting on a panel at a parenting conference hosted by the Huffington Post. Wambach is a retired American soccer player, two-time Olympic gold medalist, and FIFA Women's World Cup champion. Wambach played for the United States national soccer team from 2003 to 2015. In 2015, she was listed by Time Magazine as one of the 100 most influential people in the world.*

**Albrecht:** I am here with…
**Wambach:** Abby Wambach.
**Albrecht:** Okay, how would you define yourself?
**Wambach:** Ahhh, good question. I would say that I am a lover of all things fun. I am a Rochestarian. Hotdogs are my favorite food. I happened to play soccer on the Women's National Team for a bunch of years. I am an Olympian, a World Cup champion, and a businesswoman, a speaker, an activist, a philanthropist, and most of all, best of all, a wife and mother of three kids.
**Albrecht:** That's wonderful, one straightforward question, you're 38?
**Wambach:** I am, yeah.
**Albrecht:** Ok, looking back over the 38 years, who's your favorite teacher?

**Wambach:** My favorite teacher... well, my favorite coach is Kathleen Boughton, for sure, and I think that all coaches are teachers also. Ummm, I had a teacher in 4th grade. Her name was Mrs. Sears. She taught me about behavior and how behavior... we had a behavior star chart; if you got a compliment, you got a star. She taught me that good behavior and the way that a whole group operates collectively, you can achieve more, and so those seeds were implanted in me as a really young child. I'm part of a big family, I have been part of teams throughout my life, and because of seeing this done in a school environment, it really had a massive impact on me. I still have that as a tenant of who I am as a person, that I think that we all collectively rise when we all can operate under the same guides and on the same page. It doesn't always mean that we are going in the right direction. It doesn't mean we're on the right page, but if we're all on the same page, I think that it is super important to affect the most positive change or reach any high-level goal you're looking for. You can't do it alone.

**(interruption)**

**Albrecht:** Coach Boughton was coaching basketball over at Mercy High School?

**Wambach:** Yes, basketball and soccer. She was the best, and she was the best at teaching life, and of course, she was great at the Xs and Os. When you're that young, nobody really knows what they're doing. High school sports are so terrible anyway that it doesn't matter what you're doing on the field, but I learned about team, and what it truly meant to come together as a team from her coaching style.

**Albrecht:** Give me three words that describe Mrs. Sears...
**Wambach:** Three words... fun, challenging, and... what's the world for not belittling, when she treated us not like children?
**Albrecht:** Respect?
**Wambach:** Yep.

### REFLECTION:

I have listened to Abby Wambach's interview at least fifty times because of this one statement: She [Mrs. Sears] taught me that good behavior and the way that a whole group operates collectively, you can achieve more. When I interviewed Wambach, I initially guessed that she would identify a coach as her favorite teacher, and for a moment, she did. She credited Coach Boughton. However, under Coach Boughton, Wambach won many basketball and soccer championships. It is easy to have exceptional memories when things are going well.

Mrs. Sears had a star chart where all the students could see whether things were going well or not. This was a behavior system. The lessons she taught through the star chart revolved around how the collective positive behavior of each student led to the success of the class. When watching Wambach play soccer, it is clear that she can elevate a team; she was the captain of the Olympic gold medal and the FIFA Women's World Cup championship teams. She credits the lesson of team building to her fourth-grade teacher, Mrs. Sears.

Wambach embraces challenges. She is a world-class athlete. I was not surprised when she used the word challenging to describe Mrs. Sears. Great teachers match what they give to their students based on each of their students' needs. Wambach loves to be challenged, and Mrs. Sears most likely recognized this. The unknown is whether Mrs. Sears changed with each one of her students based on their needs. I would guess that this was the case based on Wambach's third description. Though I offered the word respect to Wambach, she described Mrs. Sears as not belittling. To belittle a person is to make them feel smaller than they should.

The first forty days of school make or break a school year. I have taught in a consultant teacher model classroom for over two decades. (A consultant teacher model classroom is a fancy way of saying that students with physical and cognitive disabilities are included with the general education population.) At the opening of the school year, priority number one is to form relationships with my students so that they build confidence. However, equally important is that I facilitate and create frequent and predictable moments in which the students get comfortable and empathetic with one another.

Building empathy between students is a necessity for developing cohesiveness. It takes more than a few icebreakers to build unity. For a minimum of forty days of school, lessons in my classroom that recognize the uniqueness of each student are explicitly taught. Once students know each other, empathy takes over, and the class begins to teach itself. Each student that is succeeding feels an obligation of service for the student that is not and immediately works with them to help clarify whatever it is that we are working on. A two-way street focused on communication and understanding is taught. Students who struggle are prepared to accept help. There is often an initial reluctance for students to accept help. Like Mrs. Sears, I have a reward system in place that recognizes small moments that guide us to understand—*All for one, and one for all.*

In the fall of 2013, I met my new fourth grade class. One of the students had been born with spina bifida. She had no feeling in her body from the waist down and was only mobile using a wheelchair or arm crutches. That student loves baseball, and she played Challenger Baseball for our town. This is a specially designed baseball program where children and adolescents play a modified version of assisted baseball.

Each student has a variety of goals and dreams. If I want to know my students' aspirations, sometimes it is not as simple as asking them. I must take the time to get to know each student. This student never explicitly said it, but many of her comments made it clear that she wanted to play regular baseball. Even with her disability, she always joined the class at recess to play kickball.

If I wanted her to feel any success, it would have to be a team effort. At recess, she began working on throwing a baseball by sitting on top of a five-gallon bucket. With some guidance from our adaptive physical education teacher and a lot of practice throwing with many students in our class, she was getting the hang of it.

I called the Rochester Red Wings, the AAA baseball farm team for the Minnesota Twins. After all her hard work, it was time to put my student on the field to throw out the opening pitch for a professional team. At first, the ball club answered, "No." As it turned out, opening pitches were reserved for sponsors. This, of course, was not acceptable. All the money in the world cannot replace the dreams of a child. I was persistent, and the Red Wings caved. In the end, they benefitted too. I did not anticipate that over 200 people from our school and town would attend the game.

Mrs. Sears taught about how ethical behavior and whole group collaboration causes an increase in achievement; this was certainly a 'Mrs. Sears moment.' When my student threw that ball fifty feet to a professional catcher, it did not matter one bit that it took a bounce before it reached home plate. What mattered was that she was on the field. When she threw that baseball, I was standing next to her grandfather, and the crowd roared! It is the first time I had ever had a grandfather cry into my shoulder. We were a family.

As chapter one of this book begins, remember that most successful people had catalysts for their success. Chapter one begins in Reggio, Italy. It is a place of beholden beauty. Its educational systems, economy and social well-being are strong. To get to this point, like Wambach or my student, human guidance had to be present to bring out the best in this town.

# Chapter 1
## Common Threads, Core Values & Innovation

(1)

THE CITY OF Reggio Emilia is nestled in northern Italy. It is directly in the heart of a triangle created between Venice, Florence, and Milan. The oldest part of the town is hexagonal in shape and surrounded by ancient walls, with the earliest construction dating back to the 16th–17th centuries. Rocky foothills surround the town.

A 5th-century resident named San Prospero is their patron saint. He embraced savoring a life of prosperity and charity. The streets resemble those of Tuscany. Over the centuries, many empires have inhabited the city, including the Phoenicians, the Trojans, and the Byzantines. As a result, the city has been reconstructed many times, with each new occupation adding its architectural style. In the 15th century, Jews fled to Reggio Emilia from Spain, Portugal, and minute pockets of Europe to escape persecution. Though World War II caused a decline in the Jewish population, there remains a modest religious influence. Tourism attracts millions of people to the city each year to relish in the rolling hills and mountains. Worldwide, Reggio Emilia is recognized for its parmesan cheese and Lambrusco wine, and Max Mara (one of Europe's globally recognized fashion designers) is headquartered there. Reggio Emelia is a joyful and prosperous city, a far cry from its status following the destruction of World War II.

The consequences of the World War II left the city and the hearts of the residents devastated. Because Reggio Emelia is in the north, it saw numerous occupations. After four long years of fighting, the Armistice of Cassibile was signed on August 3rd, 1943. The armistice stipulated the surrender of Italy to the Allies. Its stipulations forgave many of the crimes committed during the war, which did not go over well with Italians. Italians had many ideas about how their country should be rebuilt militarily, socially, and politically. There was a division over whether Italy should have abandoned the Axis powers, and a civil war ensued with the outspoken Benito Mussolini leading the rebellion. He was loyal to Hitler's principles. When the civil war finally stopped, Mussolini was dead, and Italy had the challenge of a steep uphill climb to rebuild. Italians had suffered nearly 500,000 casualties, or 1% of its country's total population. Survivors of the war had been traumatized. The paradise of today was pure pandemonium, depression, and confusion in 1946.

Louis Malaguzzi of Reggio Emelia was born in 1920, just in time to grow up in fascist Italy and remember six years of war that encompassed his youth. In 1939, his father sent him to study educational systems. Malaguzzi fondly focused on early childhood. In 1946, he was residing in Rome and was part of a campaign to reconstruct Italy. Malaguzzi remembered Reggio Emelia before the war. He believed that in order to restore Italy, a sound investment had to be made in the next generation, with a focus on mental health and wellness that start in early childhood.

In that same year Malaguzzi enrolled in the first post-war psychology program. Malaguzzi's new skill set, memories of prewar Reggio Emelia, and his desire to reform educational systems were a perfect match for a country trying to rebuild and overcome the effects of trauma. Malaguzzi returned home at a time when many people felt conflicted about how to rebuild their country. It was finally settled that the city of Reggio Emelia would invest its money and hearts within a new form of preschool, and Malaguzzi would be at the center of its creation. His timing, research, and memories were perfect.

The new institutions were referred to as the Reggio Emelia Schools, and focused nearly all their efforts on early childhood. Their central philosophy stressed high standards of guided exploration and inclusive values. The town recognized that even though budgets would have to be considered, the school would be the highest priority. All students of the town were welcomed, regardless of their income level. Parents were expected to contribute what they could, based on their salaries. In contrast to schools before World War II, students with disabilities were included; they were deemed to have individual rights, not special needs. The teachers at the Reggio Emelia School were trained as positive-minded learners, researchers, and facilitators of educational experiences. A strong emphasis was set on experiential and discovery learning. Central to the school was a resident artist. This was a local artisan that worked in the school and served as a facilitator for guiding child-centered creative thought. His or her purpose was to work on increasing creativity and imagination. The emotional growth of the city's youngest members was considered first. The health and joy of the children, not money, became the bottom line.

The Reggio Emelia Schools are still thriving. With their attainment, today they are well-funded. With all the documented success, it seems to be a "no-brainer" to borrow many of the philosophies of the Reggio Emelia model of education. Instead of infusing emotional health within instruction, a lot of the counseling, rehabilitation, and special services are delivered outside of the classroom, and often outside of the school. Why? Money has played a role in determining how schools are to be run, as well as the fact that the people who remember the horrors of war are gone. Special services are increasingly expensive. Money is a driving force behind many of the decisions that are made in schools of today.

If Malaguzzi's approach of emotional improvement was not developed in post-war Reggio Emelia, would the children ever have released the trauma of the war? The shock and trauma of war may have been passed along for generations, as they were in places that did not have the people or resources to create similar schools. Today, curriculum, standards, higher test scores, and career and college readiness have made the ambiguous exploration of child-centered and student-centered learning a reserved strategy that is used with a limited number of students. There is nothing wrong with schools readying students for careers and college but preparing students to be productive citizens is a much broader and deeper investment. Schools and careers fit for some people, but are schools just preparatory units for the businesses and factories? Is the goal of graduation a job, or are our institutions meant for total life development? Do we celebrate the achievement of dreams and hard work, or do we rejoice when the prescribed curriculum has been mastered? What is the bottom line of modern education?

Times have changed. Schools, governments and communities want to say that they work together, but do they? Turn on the news. Are the stories mostly positive or negative? The shifts in schools have a lot to do with this.

The Reggio Emelia formula targets early childhood, and it makes sense. The first years of life hold the most significant degree of physical, emotional, and cognitive development. Discovery allows for creative thought to emerge. At a stage when the language acquisition device (LAD) is at its highest, immersion in multiple forms of communication has a lasting effect. The human brain goes through many changes in its lifetime. First proposed by Noam Chomsky in the 1960s, the LAD is strictly based on theory. Essentially, a child from infancy and into childhood absorbs language much easier than an adult. The acknowledgement of LAD research is the basis for the importance of reading to children, even in infancy. As a person matures, their ability to acquire language slows. My classroom community is a melting pot of early childhood experiences. I most likely have taught only about ten students that attended a Reggio Emelia School. Unfortunately, the numbers are low because a Reggio Emelia School education is quite expensive.

There are common patterns within the cohort of Reggio Emelia taught students. Cognitively, I have observed an increase in their earlier development of higher order thinking. Reggio Emelia students independently assess social situations and are quicker to make connections and analogies. Generally, these students can freely and creatively problem solve. 100% of these students also choose to read for pleasure. Though I can only hypothesize as to why, the sensitivity to the multiple ways that children communicate, at a minimum, allows for a greater exposure to language in a variety of forms. These children have healthy ways of resolving conflict, tend to be highly empathetic, and (whether loud or shy) have a high degree of curiosity.

(2)

FOUNDED IN 1867, The National Center for Educational Statistics (NCES) is a commission within the United States Department of Education's Institute of Education Sciences. For over 150 years they have been collecting, analyzing, and reporting on educational statistics. This agency also conducts international comparisons of education statistics. The volume of data that the NCES collects and houses is massive. Their data banks include, but are not limited to, information on elementary and secondary education, libraries, assessments, early childhood, vocational aggregates, and colleges.

The purpose of investments is to take something that is being held, such as money or time, and exchange it for something that is believed to grow in value. Throughout people's lives, there are a few instances in which investments are significant. Some investments depreciate slowly, such as a car. However, most homeowners hope that their house will rise in value over time. Homes, cars, weddings, and large cash investments are often the most significant purchases that people will make. College is a substantial investment; the payout is indirect with the hope that the acquired skills and knowledge will pay off in employment. Very few investments come with a guarantee.

In the fall of 2018, nearly twenty million students attended American colleges and universities. That is an increase of about 5.1 million people since the fall of 2000. According to the NCES, in the 2000-2001 school year, a first-year college student in the United States could expect to pay on average $11,776 annually at a public institution and $21,856 at a private college. A student entering a university in 2016 could expect to pay $19,488 at a public institution and $41,468 at a private school. On a low end, a four-year degree at a public college for a student attending in the fall of 2000 would cost a bottom line of $47,104 per year, and in 2016 the average private school student could expect to pay $165,872 for a 4-year degree. College is costly and a very significant investment that twenty million students annually are going to make.

Hypothetically, if a person was buying a house, would that person haphazardly roll the dice between a ranch-style home and a colonial? Most likely not. When purchasing the house, the buyer knows that this is going to be an extraordinary investment. That buyer takes their time to evaluate the neighborhood, the age of the house, possibly the school system, the conditions of the house, and upgrades made to the home. So, does it make sense to execute a 4-year investment with an approximate cost somewhere between $50,000 and $200,000 without responsible research? How does that preparation look? What needs to be in place so that the 4-year college investment results in a successful outcome, and what role does economic status play in the decision?

The total cost of a 4-year degree is closely equivalent to that of a house. From a financial standpoint, a new homeowner does not want to buy a house with unanticipated problems and expenses. By comparison, shouldn't there be the same amount of time and exploration made when investing in a college experience? College exposes students to new ideas, challenges, and learning experiences that open a student's mind to things that may not have been previously considered. Though many students go to college with a planned major, the experience of going to college is an intermediate step between high school and independence. A lot is learned outside of the classroom. Even though it would be an ideal practice to send a student to college understanding what he or she wants to study, most studies indicate that 50% of college students will switch their major at least once. Many high schools spend time trying to help their students have a plan for what they want to study. We are hashing and rehashing a plan in high school that, with all likelihood, will change in college.

As a teacher, I have had the opportunity to watch hundreds of my students grow into adulthood. I speak with many of them regularly. Some of those students go on to college. Ideally, I would like to say that all the students who have gone to college have had a successful experience. Some have, and some have not. The following is a true story (other than the name) about one of my former students whom I communicate with regularly. It is not unique.

Noah is a brilliant young man who currently works at a favorite pizza restaurant in our hometown. Growing up, Noah was highly talented and skilled in math, loved science, and was proficient in writing. Noah mirrored the positive practices of his parents, both of whom are teachers, and his grades were rock solid. He seemed highly intelligent because he had mastered the skills on which he focused. However, he lived in the box of mastering the curriculum that was presented to him and did exactly what his teachers required. Noah continued through our public school system, graduated with excellent grades, fared in the 90th percentile on the SAT, and soon was enrolled at an Ivy League school. By all measures and standards, Noah was headed down the path of success. Noah was enrolled in the chemistry program, but after experiencing a near nervous breakdown, he dropped out in his first year. What happened?

Current American schools advocate for career and college readiness, but not all students heading into higher education are prepared. Less than 27 percent of the jobs in the United States currently require workers to possess more than a high school diploma. The Bureau of Labor Statistics (BLS), the premier government source for information on jobs, shows that only 27 percent of jobs in the U.S. economy currently require a college degree (associate degree or higher). By comparison, current surveys conducted by the United States Census Bureau, show that 47 percent of workers have an associate degree or higher. The BLS projections to 2022 forecast that the number of overqualified and underemployed college graduates will only change slightly. According to the BLS, the United States economy will create 50.6 million job openings by 2022, but only 27.1 percent of those jobs will require college degrees. That's a projected increase of only 2.1 percentage points since 1996.

Schools brag about the high percentages of students who are college bound, but according to the percentages, it seems that the bragging rights of schools are not appropriately matched to the demands of the workforce. Our workforce is over-educated for the jobs they have to perform. Going to college does not guarantee success. However, a college education allows for the possibility of career advancement. This is a delicate line to walk. There is a general sense of limitation when a student decides to stop their education at high school. Why is that? There is an American certainty that college is equated with success. However, in today's world, a growing number of college graduates are learning that a college education can lead to increased debt and difficulties finding employment.

Though each person is born with natural tendencies, a lot of what individuals become is developed through the nurturing they have received. The experiences people have as they grow have an impact on their entire lives. Noah had involved parents who expected their son to be academically successful. Noah's nurturing was healthy. He lived in a loving and stable home. After leaving school, he moved back there and is now over thirty years old living with his parents. Why did Noah fall apart at that Ivy League school? Today's educational system expects that students are to achieve a set of universal standards. These standards are designed to make an adolescent career and college ready. However, to allow students to live a life of fulfillment, the curriculum that is developed from the standards must be tailored to the student, not the system. This can be an expensive and exhausting endeavor because this approach advocates for every child to receive an individualized education, but the path to success is never easy.

At a young age, Noah lacked organizational skills and struggled with keeping a schedule. Noah was cheerful in high school, but what was not valued on paper were his social challenges. No curriculum or educator addressed this. Noah focused heavily on school and spent most of his time insulated by his family. He never experienced failure. His life experience was a lot like a baseball player only learning how to hit a baseball because that was all the coach required of that player. At some point, if a ballplayer is going to make it to the big leagues, they must learn how to field a grounder. Noah was bright, and he never received the gift of failure. When he went to college, he was surrounded by many people as talented as he was. With so many naturally talented students, he did not stand out in college. He now was required to think outside of the box that he lived in when he attended high school. Noah fell flat on his face. He was not prepared to be resilient.

In June of 2013, the New York Times published an article entitled, "Dropping Out of College, and Paying the Price." The article made the case that the increasing cost of college is a crucial factor for students leaving college. A dropout leaves school without a degree but with the potential of financial debt. This is a failed investment. The article cited that many United States students are entering college behind international students in reading and math and place the blame on poor academic preparation. Because of the simplicity of correlating educational data with dropout rates, it is a lot easier to infer that costs and preparation are the only factors when placing blame for dropping out of college. However, there are many cases, like Noah's, that buck this notion. Noah was academically ready for college, and he had earned enough scholarship money so that there was going to be little to no debt after college. It was the unmeasured factors in his life that led him to drop out.

In 1973, the United States Army created the United States Army Forces Command. Its goal was to create a tailored program to provide officers with the required skills to be decisive over a broad variety of military operations. Within this program, they did offer hard skill training on the academic jobs of military personnel, but they developed soft skills too. Soft skills are a complex variety of human social skills in the affective/social domain of people, including the way we communicate, our attitude, the approach a person takes when understanding and responding to a social situation, emotional regulation, and self-control. Common sense, a positive attitude, and flexibility are all soft skills. The United States Army acknowledged that success is developed by teaching and developing both hard and soft skills. The program was highly successful.

Why do students drop out of college? Are early exits caused by the rigor of the academics, or the student's ability to handle the new challenges in college? I would argue that the absence of soft skill development causes a critical impact on the dropout rate. If a child has never spent significant time away from home, and is suddenly living in a dorm in college, the challenges of homesickness may be felt for the first time. This is compounded with new responsibilities, becoming used to living with new people, and independently keeping a schedule. Students must be self-reliant when reading social situations and resilient when failing to meet their expectations. A student must rely heavily on their soft skills to navigate the social and emotional hurdles of the collegiate setting. What if these skills have not been developed or practiced before college? Like Noah, the student struggles, and the potential for dropping out goes up.

(3)

RAYMOND (RAY) ALBERT KROC was a high school dropout. Born in 1902, he stopped going to school at the age of 15 with the hopes of becoming a World War I Red Cross ambulance driver. When he died in 1984, Kroc was the majority owner of the San Diego Padres baseball team and had amassed over 500 million dollars as the principal owner of McDonald's Corporation. In the year 2000, Kroc was listed as one of Time Magazine's 100 most influential people of the 20th century. Like many high school dropouts, Kroc spent considerable time employed at many different jobs. He sold paper cups, played as a jazz musician, and was a disc jockey at WGES radio station near Chicago. There was a point that he bartered work at a restaurant for room and board.

In the early 1950s, Kroc was selling Hamilton Beach food mixers. He realized that people liked to pay less for comparable products. Prince Castle Mixers, which were the top-notch mixers of the day, were facing declining sales because Hamilton Beach mixers were selling at a lower price point. Kroc knew this and took note when two brothers, Richard and Maurice McDonald, bought eight of his Hamilton Beach mixers. Large purchases often equated to developing success and rapid growth, so Kroc investigated to see who these McDonald brothers were.

The McDonald brothers had set up hamburger restaurants around San Bernardino, California. Kroc visited their operation to see their restaurants firsthand. He was immediately convinced that this company had massive potential for considerable and wide scale expansion. The timing could not have been better. The brothers were searching for a franchise partner after their original partner, Bill Tansey, died. In 1954, Kroc opened the first McDonald's Systems, Inc. restaurant in Des Plaines, Illinois, the community where he grew up. Business boomed, and Kroc had dreams of expansion. Kroc envisioned franchising out to investors, while the McDonald brothers had no desire for development. Kroc's frustration turned into a proposal to buy out the McDonald brothers. In 1961, Kroc paid 2.7 million dollars for the business. No papers were signed; just a simple handshake was made. This caused problems when it came time to divide up the assets. The McDonald brothers turned the restaurants over to the employees. However, this was minor compared to the "American Dream" into which this enterprise eventually would morph. An icon of American fast food was born.

At age fifty-two, Kroc had created a financially successful chain of restaurants. This was thirty-seven years after he attended his last class in school. It would seem the odds were against him because he did not attend college, but the probabilities were also against the people of Reggio Emelia, Italy following World War

II. Kroc's parents were immigrants from Bohemia, which is now the Czech Republic. He was raised to value the soft skill of work ethic and understood how to be resilient in the face of challenges. He also insisted on the highest quality of food products. When Kroc was presented with the possibility of utilizing soybean fiber in his meat patties as a cost-cutting measure, he rejected it. Kroc standardized assembly systems that are still in place at McDonald's restaurants today. Franchises were obligated to adhere to his strict measurements and guidelines. The first franchise outside of Chicago, for example, had to tolerate Kroc's constant phone calls to management when he noticed even a smudge on the door. Kroc continued to develop an empire with his high expectations.

With all the wealth Kroc had amassed, in 1974 he bought the San Diego Padres. His team faced an opening day loss of 9-5 to the Houston Astros. In front of his 39,000+ fans, he got on the public address system and announced, "I've never seen such stupid ball-playing in all my life!" That year, with a disastrous 102 losses, the Padres drew in over 1,000,000 fans, up from the 644,772 fans they attracted in 1973. Kroc believed in a quality team for the Padres fans, and he was a consumer-friendly owner. He was not afraid to call out and fix things that were not up to his standards. Did Ray Kroc need strong math, reading, and writing skills? What were the essential skills that he required to be successful? Kroc understood customer satisfaction, resilience, and work ethic, and he was a visionary.

Later in Kroc's life, he did what many philanthropists do: he applied his money to the welfare of people. He established the

Ronald McDonald House Foundation. Its headquarters remain in Oak Brook, Illinois (Kroc's home), and the foundation has continued to grow. In 2019, 365 Ronald McDonald Houses existed worldwide. The mission of the Ronald McDonald House Foundation is to provide families of sick children with a place of support. The program has expanded to Ronald McDonald's Care Mobiles. They contribute money to provide affordable healthcare and dental work for disadvantaged children. The program has grown to serve over 100,000 children per year. Ronald McDonald Houses are most abundant in the United States, but in 1981 the first international Ronald McDonald House was opened in Toronto, Canada. Today Ronald McDonald Houses are in Australia, Bangkok, Caracas, and many other corners of the globe.

Does a person need a college education to understand the difference between an ordinary commodity and a quality product? Does a college education ensure work ethic and resilience? Where does the ambition to be charitable originate? A sound educational system will address these questions. However, these soft skills should be taught or reinforced in a home or a community. Most of these qualities are instilled in the home or set in motion by mentors. Kroc was lucky. He had parents who imparted these skills to him at an early age.

Does a person need to have a college education to be a risk-taker or a visionary? Of course, Ray Kroc's example works well when pioneering a business, and presumably would not be the best route to take as a surgeon who relies heavily on both hard skills and soft skills. An examination of what jobs are available and the skills that are in high demand that do not require a high level of education will show that Kroc was highly qualified for the time. He possessed a strong work ethic, vision, excellence, ambition, and bold honesty. Where should these skills be taught?

The Reggio Emelia schools teach and practice everything that made Kroc successful: work ethic, grit, attention to detail, and quality products for the customer. If the school and the community are highly involved with each other, then the values children learn will be similar in all aspects of their lives. Do communities and businesses work closely with their schools? Are the values shared? Children are a dipstick of the health of schools and communities when evaluating how successful the communities are. When the values of the school and the community are in full alignment, students hear consistent messages. The most potent alliances provide students with the highest potential for success.

(4)

IN 1829, CHARLES BOWLES was born in Norfolk, England. Two-year-old Charles's family immigrated to Jefferson County, New York. Bowles grew up in the historic Alexandria Bay section of New York City. He, like Ray Kroc, would be closely associated with the immigration movement of millions of people moving from Europe to America. By all accounts, Bowles excelled in school, was well dressed, and responsible. He often wore a wool dress coat and kept his hair trimmed neatly. In a crowd of people, Bowles would not stick out. Instead, he would blend into the sea of people like the small pebbles molded in a concrete sidewalk.

However, on the inside, Charles Bowles was a man of vision and adventure. At age twenty, he and his two brothers learned that something extraordinary was being discovered 3,000 miles away in California: gold. With little hesitation, the three Bowles brothers packed up their gear and began a trek westward. Tragedy struck when the brothers became ill and died, leaving Charles to mine on his own. For two years, Bowles mined the North Fork of the American River in California. Mining proved to be a hopeless cause, and around 1852, Bowles left California and settled in Decatur, Illinois where he married and had four children.

So far, there is nothing extraordinary about Charles Bowles. He had a failed business venture, but this was nothing too unusual. Bowles was resilient. In April of 1861, the American Civil War erupted, and by August of 1863, Bowles enlisted in the B Company of the 116th Illinois Regiment as a private. He fought and was wounded in the Battle of Vicksburg. Subsequently, he was part of Sherman's March to the Sea, and in April of 1865, near the end of the Civil War, he was discharged at the rank of First Lieutenant. Upon his release, Bowles returned to Illinois.

Gold fever never left Charles Bowles, as it did not for so many people. So, unsurprisingly, in 1867 he moved his family and life in Illinois to prospect in the hills of Montana. He often wrote home. One day a letter arrived addressed to his wife about a dispute he had had with the Wells Fargo Bank. That would be the last letter she would receive. Bowles abruptly disappeared off the face of the earth. No more letters appeared, and his wife, Mary Elizabeth, assumed that he died, which was a common occurrence for the period. Bowles had become dust in the wind.

Fast forward 16 years, and Charles emerged from the shadows with a name change: Charles Bart, a prisoner. What ensued between the years of 1875 to 1883 makes for a great bedtime story that could shape and create imagination and curiosity. What is fascinating about Bowles is not necessarily why he was arrested, but the circumstances of his character upon arrest. He went from being a family man, to a gold prospector, to an eventual prisoner. Like Ray Kroc, timing would play a key role in Charles Bowles' story. From 1875 on, Charles Bowles was the infamous stagecoach robber known by the press as Black Bart. His name was contrived by the media due to the black hood he donned during his string of assaults on mostly Wells Fargo armored wagons.

As Black Bart's folk hero status grew, the news reported that he was leaving behind poetic messages to his living victims. In the media, Bowles appeared vicious, though he never harmed a soul. He was appreciated as an oxymoronic "gentleman bandit." When he robbed a stagecoach, he did not use foul language, and though he carried a shotgun, he never fired it. Bowles claimed to have people hiding in bushes ready to shoot, but ironically it was discovered on many occasions that Bowles had fashioned sticks to look like guns. Bowles was persuasive and very deceptive. These are soft skills.

Charles Bowles, Ray Kroc, and the Reggio Emelia schools are all success stories, and they provide us with insight into what success is. The path to success is a lot like traveling to a city. There are many roads that take you there. Most people travel by highway, but some people take side roads. Then, there are those that create their own new path and find new ways to reach the city. These people are the creators of unconventional success. The combination of Bowles, Kroc, and the Reggio Emelia schools share a common thread that weaves their stories together. Their path to success was original. In the case of Bowles, he let the media create a frenzy that built people's perception of him to be menacing, though he was not. Kroc was different. He recognized trends for high quality fast food and capitalized on it. The Reggio Emelia schools also saw a need to rebuild mental health through schools. All three examples prove that there are many unconventional paths to success waiting to be discovered.

(5)

CORE VALUES ARE only valuable if people appreciate them. There is a correlation between positive core values and an increased impact on community needs. Communities all over the world have large populations of impoverished and malnourished families. In the same population, some well-off families embrace charity. The concept of giving is valued and ingrained in their family. As a result, money, time, and food donations are made throughout the year. When community needs are high, the impact of a core value that fulfills that need is precious.

In the 1990s, I spent many college spring breaks living at the St. Francis House in the Kensington section of Philadelphia. Kensington has challenges. There are drug issues, poverty, and hunger. The St. Francis Home runs a daily open-door free meal service for the community around lunchtime. Early each month, the kitchen may serve one hundred and twenty meals per day. However, as the month progresses, the line at the soup kitchen grows longer. The reason for this is pretty simple. The welfare checks arrive early in the month. By mid-month, the money runs out, and people need to eat. The increase in need is met by the Franciscan's core value to feed the hungry without question.

What were the needs of Italy in post-World War II, specifically in Reggio Emelia? Who was best equipped to address those needs? Needs and core values operate together something like a jigsaw puzzle. Almost every piece in a puzzle can be forced unnaturally together, but the imperfect fit eventually will be evident as a flaw in the puzzle. In a thriving environment, the pieces fit. If parts are forced, they can be irreversibly damaged. Often, when we construct a puzzle and search for the right piece, we must search through a lot of similar pieces and try a few that appear correct. Then, ultimate satisfaction is received when a puzzle piece falls into place. It takes patience, time, and careful observation.

Is a puzzle constructed by systematically trying to fit each piece with every piece one at a time? It would work, but it is not logical. A puzzle builder will look for matching colors, a distinct mark shared by two pieces, or the general shape of the piece. Subconsciously, a puzzle-builder has multiple strategies working simultaneously. If he or she remains on a one-track system trying every piece until a match is made, a lot of wasted time will go by and often the puzzle will stay incomplete. Strategies help the puzzle builder come closer to finding a match. A puzzle builder is an active and focused observer of what he or she is trying to build.

The way a puzzle is constructed and the path to solving the complex challenges of a community are similar. When needs and core values fit within a society, like well fit puzzle pieces, everything from happiness to health prospers. A tight-knit community is precisely what allowed for the existence of unconventional success in the case of Reggio Emelia, Italy.

Post-World War II Italy had many needs. At the time, subjects like post-traumatic stress disorder, mental illness, and relationships were not as understood as they are today. Those men who survived the World War most likely also fought in the Italian Civil War. Families in Italy not only lost husbands and fathers but suffered through occupations, air raids, and bore witness to death and destruction. Children who witnessed the horrors of war were shaped by experiences, intellect, and a general understanding of the world based on the experiences that they had been through. Like the allegorical cave Plato refers to in *The Republic*, people develop through what they witness. In Plato's book, a person is shown images on a cave wall for a very long time. Those images shape the human being that they are to become. Plato knew this 3,000 years ago, and psychologists know this today. Each person is born with a nature, but the experiences a person has will shape their character too.

The needs of children in Italy following the war were diverse. Fundamentally, the aggressive way of life that existed during World War II had carried away the soft skills of expression, creativity, and the joy of random play. Louis Malaguzzi recognized this, but he cannot be credited solely with the development of the Reggio

Emelia approach to early childhood education. He worked with the people of Reggio Emelia and the surrounding towns to develop a unique and innovative learning environment for young children. Malaguzzi was in synchronicity with the people of the community. He conceded to wherever they were in their lives and understood what they had absorbed through a world war and a civil war.

Malaguzzi focused his efforts on the primary ages. He realized that if a person was suffering because of war, residual depression, frustration, fear, and anger would be unconsciously passed on and learned by the next generation. Malaguzzi understood the significance of early childhood intervention and its benefit to help the youngest members of their community to process their emotions and experiences accordingly. According to the North American Reggio Emelia Alliance, the post-World War II sentiment was a "desire to bring change and create a new, more just world, free from oppression, urging women and men to gather their strength and build with their own hands, schools for their young children." The Reggio Emelia school model spread worldwide. These schools develop values based on community needs and wants.

Traditional American educational systems streamline individual expression; universal and current systems dictate a set curriculum. On the other hand, children within a Reggio Emelia school are encouraged to be leaders of education. Though schools have standards and benchmarks, the culture in a Reggio Emelia school is entirely centered on the interest of the child.

This chapter began with an interview of Abby Wambach. Wambach stressed that if a group is going to be successful, all the participants need to be on the same page and going in the same direction. She acknowledged that sometimes groups may not be on the right page or going the correct way, but she stressed that cohesiveness outweighs perfection. For the Reggio Emelia Schools to succeed, they had to act like a successful Olympic soccer team.

Admittedly, the Reggio Emelia model was designed for early childhood. As students get older, there is a need for some standardization of skills. Unfortunately, what can be lost in the process is the need for an individualized education based on needs and interests. However, as students grow older, they are at different developmental stages; therefore, a more structured educational approach is appropriate. The early childhood methods of the Reggio Emelia Schools allow for a child to feel a sense of control over the direction of their learning. Think back to the insufficiencies of Reggio Emelia. The school was founded by people who knew Reggio Emelia because they lived there, and after World War II, the citizens had a feeling of lost control. The Reggio Emelia School was a new beginning and a replacement for the void. Community involvement energized that further. The teachers at Reggio Emelia schools are not guided by a set curriculum, a set scope, or a sequence of lessons, but instead are well-versed in communication between educators to allow for shared learning and exploration to occur in synchronicity with the empowered children. Established standards are achieved through child-centered lessons and evolving curriculums.

Children at a Reggio Emelia school learn through varied experiences involving touching, moving, hearing, seeing, and exploration. Malaguzzi believed that young children had over a hundred different "languages" of communication; knowing this, it makes sense that children are encouraged to interact with other children through their own "language". They feel a sense of freedom of expression and empowerment when the only boundary that exists is to treat others with dignity and respect.

What are the vital soft skills that are taught at such an early age? In the gap left by the war, there was little to no interaction between children. If the communication between children is stunted at the earliest ages, will that child grow to become an adult who trusts their peers, communicates well, and has tolerance for others? Probably not. The simple concept of interaction, separate from a formal setting, allowed for children attending the Reggio Emelia Schools to learn how to communicate and trust one another. It seems natural and obvious that students should be interacting at school, but years of war had created a cloud of distrust. Fundamental human interaction was absent. When visiting a Reggio Emelia School, it is not unusual to find children under four carrying on conversations with adults. There is a striking sense of confidence within each child.

A child at a Reggio Emelia School feels empowerment over their learning. For many, this is tough to imagine because traditional schooling puts the teacher in charge of direct instruction. The traditional education in the western world has the curriculum being delivered through the teacher as the central facilitator of the lesson. Under this format of training, the learners have limited control over what they are learning. One way to imagine this shift of educational "power" is to understand its parallel to apprenticeships. An apprentice chooses what they want to learn by working with a master artisan. Though the apprentice will closely mimic the skills of the master (or facilitator of learning), they will take on a unique style as they continue to learn. A path may be chosen, but creativity is not ignored.

A Reggio Emelia approach is like a group of apprentices learning and communicating together, each honing their craft while being encouraged to share with their peers and elders. The master craftsman does not sit back but rather works alongside the apprentices. In Italy post 1945, people had lived under a strict military structure. Due to occupations by other countries, they had no control, and the Reggio Emelia School filled that void.

Citizens were able to take back control by contributing to the school as a community. The current structure dictates that businesses, government, parents, and community members are expected to participate in the school. In fact, in Reggio Emelia, there is a citizen action council called La Consulta that has many educated members. This group influences the local government. With the Reggio Emelia School focused so heavily on community and parent interaction, it is clear why the government listens.

Remember Noah? He elected to leave his Ivy League university to work at a pizza parlor. It can only be speculated what impact a child-centered educational approach would have had on his future. Noah's story is not unique. According to the *Chronicle of Higher Education*, an online journal that investigates real-world data supported by funding through the Bill and Melinda Gates Foundation, this is our reality. The Chronicle examined 3,600 leading public colleges and universities in the United States. In 2013, The University of Virginia posted the highest graduation rate from a 4-year school at 86.3%. This means that at America's top graduating university, 13.6% of college students failed to finish a 4-year degree in four years. 71.2% of students of color completed their 4-year degree in four years.

The University of Michigan is ranked second on this list. After four years, 75.8% of students eligible to graduate with a 4-year degree finished in four years. Black minorities underperformed the average at a staggering 58.8%. What happened to the students who did not complete their 4-year degree? In the case of the University of Michigan, 90% of these students did complete their 4-year degree in six years. This delay adds a significant increase to the cost of the degree. 90% still sounds good until the realizations that 10% of the population failed. That 10% represents real people and is not a small percentage by any means. According to the University of Michigan's website, the 2016 out-of-state tuition was $43,476. This cost does not include room, board, or living expenses. Similarly, the University of Virginia's 2016 tuition cost was $43,822. Remember, Virginia and Michigan are at the top of graduation rates.

In 2013, just 38.7% of all the students surveyed nationally graduated with a 4-year degree in four years. 59.2% managed to get a degree in six years. The national average expenditure after aid packages for a four-year degree was $71,334. Costs for private colleges were significantly higher, but the most shocking statistics were in community colleges. New York State has thirty-five community colleges as part of their State University of New York (SUNY) system. After surveying 61,751 New York students in 2013 who started their college career at a community college, only 20.6 percent graduated with a 2-year degree. Of the subcategories, only 11.7 percent of black attendees graduated within the anticipated two years. This is par for the course nationally.

Should everybody go to college? Should even a large population of students go to college? Is college necessary? With college costs being so high, these economic statistics cannot be ignored from either an economic standpoint or a perspective of readiness.

(6)

SUCCESS CREATES PATTERNS. There is comfort in predictability, and consequently, most people lock into set fashions, routines, family activities, and careers. In the 1990s, the Search Institute, an independent mid-western research organization, concluded a study of over four million children. The focus of the study was not attempting to unlock the secret of becoming rich, employed, or famous. At the core of the study was an attempt to uncover the factors that play essential purposes in child development which improve the probability that the child will become a productive and healthy adult with a firm grasp on their future. Common threads of behaviors and circumstances weave through the fabric of people's experiences, and they often produce similar outcomes. The research that the Search Institute pursued was to find the threads that, when stitched early in life, have a significant impact on future success.

Nike is iconic in the corporate world of sports. They invest millions of dollars in slogan-based campaigns to catch global attention; they have launched multiple campaigns aimed at showcasing the average person. One such ad campaign was called "Greatness." As part of that campaign, a television commercial ran for several months. The camera locked on a country road. From a distance, a person was slowly jogging closer. The natural assumption was that the runner was going to be an athlete decked out in spandex or nylon running gear, but this runner was nothing of the sort. He was an overweight teenager running at a struggling pace. The visual message in the ad campaign—and the slogan that accompanied the initial phase of the campaign was "Find your greatness."

What does it mean to live a successful life? People often do not measure their success on their own. Social abnormalities are made to look like norms in advertisements. This causes many to measure themselves through comparisons made to others. Why was it so shocking to see the overweight kid in the Nike commercial? Often, societies value the product more than the process. A perfect body is valued more than the process needed to get in shape. The overweight kid is not supposed to be running, especially in something as fashionable as a pair of Nike sneakers. This commercial challenged the very essence of the limits of our self-concept.

How do we pin down the means of success? The Search Institute utilized data from a sample size of four million children to find the root causes of success. It is tough to refute or ignore any study that has a sample size of four million individuals. In 1990, the Search Institute's first results were published and have been consistently updated each year.

The Search Institute was founded in 1958 by Merton P. Strommen, Ph.D. He pioneered the use of social science to research and understand the lives, beliefs, and values of young people. Strommen has remained an innovator, listening to young people in an effort to promote positive change. His actions mirror those of the people of Reggio Emelia following World War II. The Search Institute's research is extensive. Their work is grounded in the development of heathy communities. They have multiple publications with practical school, family and community ideas, assessment tools, and websites dedicated to helping parents raise mentally and physically healthy children. In 2007, the Search Institute went global, implementing many of their practices in thirty different countries with each initiative being adapted into the native language of that country. Most recently, the Search Institute has focused on initiatives targeting adult and child relationships within a family. Their primary focus has been on early adolescence.

Today's good-hearted teachers spend much of their time in classrooms trying to impart the wealth of knowledge that exist within a curriculum. Generally, students are told to share their thoughts. However, for communication to be effective, students need to listen as well as speak, digest what they hear, and respond. Teachers need to do the same thing. With the ever-growing pressure from the media, the government, and society for children to achieve a higher academic standard, educational systems are under enormous pressure to pump children and young adults full of information. Listening takes time, patience, and for some educators, a leap of faith. However, the Search Institute is a privately funded non-governmental research institute that is not pressured by the government or organizations. They are the perfect establishment to be investigating success.

A Merriam-Webster dictionary definition of success is "the correct or desired result of an attempt." Who determines the correct result? A teacher? Society? Parents? The government? The people themselves? The students? A more in-depth look at other definitions of success defines it as the "attainment of wealth."

That would indicate that a successful person is one who accumulates money or possessions. This is one way that modern society assesses success, with the concept that he who dies with the most toys wins. According to this definition, a successful individual is not one that works hard but rather is a person who has a better bottom line.

Does money equate to success? For many years, federal and state subsidies have been poured into schools where there is a higher degree of poverty. The philosophy behind this initiative is to put more support where there is a lower income. Statistically, students who come from moderate to low income families tend to grow at a slower academic rate. According to a 2010 report on reading education by the Casey Foundation, a private charitable organization that advocates for policies to help needy children and families, 85% of American students who came from schools that are considered "high poverty schools" were below proficiency in literacy by the time they reached fourth grade.

The data is similar when disregarding the school data and looking at poverty across the board. In this case, 83% of fourth grade students from low income families in all schools are reading below proficiency. There is only a 2% difference in reading performance between high and low concentrations of schools with students in poverty. This indicates that learning achievement is not necessarily an effect of the school that a student attends but rather of resources and wealth of the home in which they live. This factor is external to schools' control, yet it is linked to poor performance. What is happening in the home, not the school, has a collective impact on reading achievement. Money is a factor that helps promote success but having money does not necessarily equal success.

Based on the examples of those people whom we see as thriving, success is defined as productive individuals who contribute back to their community, country, or world. Service to the community is also a core value of the Reggio Emelia schools. This definition is quite like what the Search Institute defines as success. According to the Search Institute, there are 40 key factors or assets, some intrinsic and some extrinsic, that cause children to become caring, responsible, and productive adults. This is how Ray Kroc and the notorious outlaw, Black Bart, developed their success. They possessed many specific assets that were established early in their lives.

(7)

As noted, Charles Bowles was an educated man turned gold miner and the legendary stagecoach robber, Black Bart. His name was used by screenwriters Bob Clark, Leah Brown, and Jean Shepherd in the 1983 movie *A Christmas Story*. The main character,

Ralphie, imagines saving his family with his Daisy Air Rifle from an assault by Black Bart and his band of thieves. There is also a fishing bait called a Black Bart. The lure is characterized by its ability to deceive fish. Hollywood and the sporting world have skewed the accuracy behind the name. Black Bart was an authentic person with a four-year string of success in the media as a criminal. Though he may not have been ethically successful, many saw him as such.

Black Bart had developed an unclear vendetta against the Wells-Fargo Bank Company. This can be assumed because shortly after he wrote his wife about an altercation with Wells-Fargo, he disappeared. He became a criminal with a vendetta; most of his targets were stagecoaches owned by Wells-Fargo. As time passed, Black Bart mythically grew to be glorified, not as a villain, but as a legend in the California newspapers. As the legend grew, a picture of Black Bart developed that paralleled a young David taking on the Goliath known as Well-Fargo.

Black Bart's robberies were not anything fancy. He would abruptly appear in the middle of a stagecoach trail. His weapons of choice were two menacing double-barreled 12-gauge shotguns. Black Bart concealed his face with a dark hood. Though he appeared as a fearsome foe, there was an almost cartoonish appearance to his character. At nearly every one of his robberies, he left an original handwritten poem. Bart grew up educated and proper by British standards. His original verses were not what you would expect from a man who has been living the life of an outlaw. Here is an example of Black Bart's work from July 25th, 1878, after he robbed a stagecoach near Quincy, California:

> Here I lay me down to Sleep
> To wait the coming morrow
> Perhaps Success perhaps defeat
> And everlasting Sorrow
> Let come what will I'll try it on
> My condition can't be worse
> And if there's money in that Box
> 'Tis munny [sic] in my purse.
> -Charles Bowles, 1878

In this robbery, Bowles made off with $379 and some jewelry, a tidy sum for 1878. Society tends to judge those people who are committing criminal acts as violent, lawless, and without morals. Many are just that. However, that is where Bart's legacy has an odd twist.

Robbery number twenty-nine did not go well. Charles Bowles was shot; he was able to escape, but the trail led an investigator to a bloody handkerchief. Like most men of the time, Bowles carried a handkerchief, even to his robberies. On the corner of each handkerchief was a laundry identification number. It turned out that Black Bart used a dry-cleaning service. After investigating over one hundred laundries, a match was made, and authorities apprehended Black Bart.

Black Bart was fictionalized by the media to be a menacing thief. However, he never once fired a shot during any of his robberies. He did not even return fire when he was shot. Once he was in custody, it was discovered that not only did Charles Bowles never load his guns, but he was also afraid of horses and always escaped authorities by foot. In the end, when he was captured, Bowles gave no struggle, nor did he give a fiery gunslinger showdown. Due to his notoriety and willingness to give back most of the money he had stolen, he received minimal punishment and was never seen or heard from again.

Good stories are beloved, especially in the media. Was Black Bart successful? Accidentally, yes. A successful individual contributes back to their community, country, or world. A thief is a criminal. However, paradoxically, in the media, Black Bart was a huge success. He was the Robin Hood of his generation, so beloved that he inspired a scene in the movie Butch Cassidy and the Sundance Kid. In that movie, Butch Cassidy wanted to get into a railroad car, so his band of thieves blew the entrance off the railcar with dynamite. Too much explosive led to an unanticipated over-detonation and blew money in the air everywhere. Cassidy was more concerned about the man inside guarding the money. He immediately looked for the man safeguarding the car. When Butch Cassidy found the man alive, he advised him that he should be getting paid more.

Black Bart's life as a thief was successful until his twenty-ninth robbery, and the public and media wildly embraced his character. This is a dichotomy that seems to be part of human nature. Most people equate popularity with success. How many of us experienced a popularity contest in high school when it came time to elect a class president? Most of the time, the popular person won the election, and that person was not necessarily the one who would create progress for the class. Perception, whether through the media or in a school, influences our decisions. It gives us a misleading belief that a popular person will promote success. It happens all the time and reduces our development and progress as a society.

(8)

JOYFUL PRODUCTIVITY EQUATES to success. It sometimes is misunderstood. The robberies of Charles Bowles illustrate that there can be points where a person is successful even though that success has been fictionalized by those who do not know the person. Gossip, the media, and Hollywood are all examples of media outlets where the tail wags the dog. This skews perception from reality. What can be done to spread the truth?

The 40 developmental assets hold much significant evidence. The research of the Search Institute is ongoing. They have identified the critical factors in a child's life that increase the probability of that child becoming successful. The framework for the assets draws on community resources and families. It begins at birth and ends at age 18. The assets are organized and presented to be applicable for early childhood, middle childhood, and adolescents. It is not a coincidence that many of the factors that the Search Institute identified parallel the Reggio Emelia schools' pedagogical priorities. By having substantial factors identified, we have a comprehensive and concrete framework for proactivity. At an early age, a child can be assessed to see how many positive assets they have out of the 40. This list allows schools, neighborhood communities, families, and religious communities to determine well-identified factors that can be worked on to guide a child into successful adulthood.

The developmental assets are divided into two categories: intrinsic and extrinsic. According to the Search Institute, "The more assets that young people have, the less likely they are to engage in a wide range of high-risk behaviors and the more likely they are to thrive. Research shows that youth with the most assets are least likely to engage in four different patterns of high-risk behavior, including problem alcohol use, violence, illicit drug use, and sexual activity. When they have a greater number of assets, they are more likely to do well in school, be civically engaged, and value diversity." The list of the developmental assets identifies factors that increase the likelihood of the eventual success or challenges of an individual. A closer look at the research on developmental assets gives us some concrete evidence about the original underlying reasons why some people struggle and why others thrive.

There are twenty external assets; external assets are those that require an outside factor. Each of these external assets is divided into one of four subcategories. The first set of assets involve the support of the people surrounding the child. These include active neighbors, supportive family members, reliable communication, confident adults in the educational setting, and active parental involvement. A central feature of the Reggio Emelia schools is parental and community involvement. Four of the external developmental assets involve the empowerment of children. The community is not only supposed to value the children but view them as resources. Again, there is a parallel with the Reggio Emelia schools. The next six external assets target boundaries. Not only do parents, adults, and caregivers provide discipline, but the child learns self-control through the guidance of the adults in their lives. Reggio Emilia schools embrace a similar philosophy. The final four external assets list the constructive use of time. The development of the child is enhanced through productive play, which encourages creativity and expression. There is also a balance between activities in the community, involvement with religious groups, and growing up in productive homes that stress work ethic. Like the assets, the Reggio Emelia schools encourage their students to explore their interests. Well-calculated planning throughout childhood produces the most significant opportunity for success.

Internal assets are those assets the child possesses that are not tangible. Though others shape them, it is the child's choice whether these assets are developed. The first five assets include the child's internal commitment to learning. They include curiosity, engagement in a variety of experiences, and the steady transfer of these skills at home or at daycare. Children with a strong commitment to learning see the relationship between their home and the school. This places a tremendous value on frequent and consistent communication between schools and homes. Success is fostered by a child who reads daily. Six assets focus on the child's system of values. Do they have integrity, responsibility, and honesty? Do they care for others and have a network of social justice? A child with a high number of assets has social competency. They can plan, resist negative temptations, cooperate, and practice peaceful conflict resolution.

The teacher is a partner with the student in the Reggio Emelia School. Like an apprenticeship, there is a meaning to modeling behaviors to help the child learn specific skills. A child is prepared for success when they have a positive identity. A child with a confident individuality can make decisions and choices, have a healthy self-concept and purpose, and possess a positive outlook on the future.

All children and adults have deficits. No person has all forty assets, and many successful people do not even have twenty-five. However, the more assets a developing child lacks, the more likely it is that they will not find success as an adult. Conversely, the more assets a child has, the higher the chance they will reach a level of success. If the characteristics of successful people are correlated with pockets of successful schools, governments, communities, and families, patterns will emerge that explain why they are thriving. Like Black Bart, what appears in the media as the truth is not always the real reason something occurred. Many people in all facets of life use statistics as the tail to wag the dog, diverting attention away from what is real by shooting from the hip as a guess for what is at the root of success or a problem.

When a school system involving all stakeholders in a community can transform part of a country from a war-torn mess to a happy and prosperous place, it cannot be ignored. Why are the developmental assets and the Reggio Emelia model for learning not universally adopted? Data proves that both models develop successful human beings. However, the impact of their approach is hard to assess. Though there is data that supports that their presence leads to success, a correlation is not as clear as the result of a math problem. Often, we blame lowered success levels on schools or poverty. The federal government spends billions of Title I dollars on education based merely on poverty rates alone. However, the foundation of what causes children to become successful is the emotional development of the child coupled with the alignment of culture. The practices and beliefs of the community have a widespread impact on the future success of children. It is apparent that a paradigm shift needs to occur in the structure and practices that guide families, communities, schools, and governments. This change will take a leap of faith. There is pressure for students to master math and literacy at an early age, but social-emotional development takes more time. What is more important: the increased amount of knowledge a student has or the development of a solid foundation that increases the probability that a child becomes a healthy adult? Children—they are the dipstick of our society to measure how well the engine is truly running.

# Interview with Sal Khan
*February 1, 2018*
*San Francisco, California*

*I met Sal Khan in San Francisco at the headquarters for Google. He was a keynote presenter and talked a lot about education. Khan founded Khan Academy, a free online education platform. Initially, he produced lessons, mostly focused on math and science, out of a tiny room in his house. According to 2019 data, Khan Academy has 4.7 million subscribers and the website's videos have been viewed over 1.6 billion times. In 2012, Time Magazine listed Khan on its annual list of the 100 most influential people in the world. The following interview is typed exactly as it was spoken. The amount that Khan jumps around reveals a lot about the experiences he had in school.*

**Albrecht:** This is a question that does not necessarily deal with Khan Academy, but I am interested in you through your thoughts, through a remarkable lens. You're a fascinating person. Who is your favorite teacher of all time? If you look back on your life, who was an influential teacher, and would you describe that teacher to me?

**Khan:** So, I would say there are three that immediately come to mind, but if I would think more, there would be about twenty, ummm. Mr. Hernandez was one of them. I think what really stood out, why he was so important to me was; he was my algebra II teacher. And, he was the advisor to the math club and the math team, but he kind of treated me like an equal. In a lot of ways, he was my mentor. He, he was a teacher, and he was kind of vulnerable, this is what I've got to do, this and that, and I had this deep empathy, and also, he believed in me. He wrote all of my recommendations for M.I.T., and there are not a lot of kids that go from Grace King to M.I.T., and he's the one who told me that, not like, I think you should apply. And, no one from our school has ever gone, so I think him for sure.

Ms. Kennedy, who was actually our journalism teacher. I was on the school newspaper, and it was a class at the high school I went to, Grace King High School, and she ran that class like a newspaper, like a real newspaper, and so, again, she treated me like a member of the team. There wasn't this separation between the teacher and the student.

If you go earlier, in second grade, and this is one of my earliest formative experiences, um, and it's funny, my sister was always the high-end achiever, and she took all of the gifted classes and all of that. I thought I was in gifted until I realized I was in speech therapy. But, because of my sister, they kept testing me. They're like that last test is fair and it's so strong, I'm serious. I don't think most kids get this opportunity to get tested. And, I eventually wound up getting into the program, and the first day I showed up, and I remember I was in second grade, and there was this weird thing where they would take you out of a different class period to go to this program. I walked into this room and there was Ms. Kraus and

Ms. Roselle, and I was seven years old and the memory is seared in my head, and it was like a classroom I had never seen before. There weren't tables in one direction. There were a bunch of kids of mixed ages all doing different things. Some kids were playing chess. Some kids were drawing, and I said, "What is this secret world that I have fallen into?"

And, they said, "You, you come here," and the teachers, they said, "What are you interested in?"

And I was like, "You're asking me? I like to draw."

"Then we'll draw."

"I like puzzles."

"Then we'll do puzzles."

And, I thought I was getting away with something, and I thought that I can't tell anyone about this. Is this some type of scam that's been going in the school? Ummm, but I really, I don't really remember a lot more about second grade, but I remember those moments.

So, I think the theme is when I was able to have human interaction and get that one-on-one time. One thing we try to do at the Lab School is every student gets at least fifteen minutes one-on-one with a teacher every week. And, it might not sound like a lot, but if we all introspect on how much those one-on-one moments with caring adults are the stuff that is seared into your head, so I think those are the teachers that have had a really big... there's also a teacher at the University of New Orleans, Dr. Hira Santinea that took me under his wing when I was in high school, and I took some courses there, and he was the one who said you should do this, you should think about this, you know. I didn't have access to a computer at my house, so he took a computer to me so I could learn how to program.

### Reflection:

When Sal Khan recalled his teachers, it became apparent that he had multiple great experiences at school. Though he did not explicitly state he felt successful every day, I am able to infer that most days he did. Khan described Mr. Hernandez as a vulnerable person who treated him like an equal and believed in him. Because of his strength in math, Khan gained the privilege to access a "secret" room in the school for gifted students where he was empowered to make choices. By providing opportunities, Khan self-inflated his strengths. He had domains where he was already thriving and received academic freedom and one-on-one time with an adult to taste additional success.

Sal Khan's recollection of his beloved teachers presents a formula for promoting success. Start with any talent. Work with that talent every day and put one adult in that skilled student's life that gives them personal attention. When that student is ready for independence, establish an opportunity where they get to determine their path of development. The student that was afforded the opportunity grows organically based on his or her nature. However, this model only works when there is time built into a school day in which every ability can be valued. The student must be held responsible too. For this opportunity, a student must combine their talent with a strong work ethic and creativity.

School districts and counties must put budgets together. They manage federal dollars, state aid, and local taxes. The objective of any school budget is to provide the best possible education and resources for the students. Test data often impacts many decisions about placement and the unique services each student receives. The tests at the state level concentrate heavily on math, reading, and writing. Daily instruction, in turn, falls in line with what is valued on the assessments. Even at the high school level, poor literacy has a significant impact on scores in content areas such as math, science, and social studies. This realization is cause for concern.

Literacy is essential. There is a significant decrease in the number of people who read for pleasure. Up until electronic devices were standard, people were carrying books or newspapers. Reading for pleasure develops focus, vocabulary, and creativity, and it increases a person's practical knowledge. With the advent of electronic devices, students and adults are mostly reading snippets of communication such as texts or emails. Fewer people are spending extended time reading. The result nationwide is that people are decreasingly literate. This is troubling.

My worries are compounded by what skills are valued in school. There is a heavy emphasis on math, reading, and writing. What is not built into the school day is the opportunity for students to develop and expand their range of talents. There is a need for all students to recognize that they are good at something and be empowered, so they feel a higher level of success. Increased success translates to an improvement in work ethic, and this develops the grit needed to tackle challenging subjects like math, reading, or writing.

Eli was in my fourth-grade class, and he was a handful. A visit to his home gave some indication as to why. He lived on a busy road with no other students. He struggled in math, reading, and writing, and he often shut down quickly if he had to do any of the three. He acted out a lot. The typical reaction to Eli's lower skill levels was to recommend special services and extra work in math by coming to school ninety minutes early to work in our Sunrise Scholars program. This was compounded with a ninety-minute block of reading instruction on top of regular English Language Arts instruction. This method of intervention made his behavior worse. The school is not to blame, since the effort level of the teachers and staff was substantial. However, even with all this support, Eli was not growing academically.

Willy was a severely cognitively challenged student. He had a full-time aide, and his day was spent developing necessary life skills. I intentionally introduced Eli to Willy. After Willy and Eli began to get to know one another, one thing became clear: Eli had deep empathy for people who have challenges. Under an aide's supervision, Eli began to read to Willy. He ate lunch and played with Willy. Never once did Eli have to be corrected when working with Willy. Eli started asking me if I would stay after school with him. He began to do his homework with me, and though his behaviors were not always perfect, he calmed down quite a bit. Eli was feeling success with Willy, and this snowballed into wanting to work after school. Eli's literacy slowly increased, and he began to see his growth. Eli's talent was valued. He had a talent, and it was working with mentally challenged students.

Positivity can spread, but so can negativity. Whenever adverse actions are chosen, negativity sets in. In Eli's case, he was stuck in a mindset when he became my student. If I wanted Eli to feel good about himself, I needed to teach him that he had the strength to go through tough things. The change in his schedule that allowed him to work with a disabled student taught Eli that it feels good to be good at something. Initially, he did not know this.

Sal Khan is not much different from my student, Eli. At first glance, any teacher that has had Eli may consider this a stretch. Khan has a website with millions of daily users. Eli gets in trouble a lot. Minus behavior, the only difference between Eli and Khan involves talent. Khan's talent is in math. Schools spend a lot of time teaching math, and therefore gifted programs were there for him to develop his drive, talent, and creativity in mathematics. Eli's talent is empathy for disadvantaged students. There are few to no schools in the country that have a gifted and talented program focused on empathy. I wonder why that is. If one existed and Eli was in that program, he would have felt a greater sense of success. The feeling of success helps people with confidence and decision making, and after years of using his gift, Eli would have developed a pattern and progress, so that gradually the areas of math, reading and writing could be addressed with higher success.

In 2017, 40% of students in grades three through eight who took the New York State English Language Arts assessment met the standard. That number rose to 45% in 2018. This means that 55% to 60% of students were told that they were not meeting the state standards. The numbers were identical in math. 40%, then 45% of students met the state standard. How does this impact the feeling of student success? It is not acceptable for students to have weak math, reading, or writing skills. If public schools are going to say, "Hey student, you are not meeting the standards," the schools need to find domains to build the confidence, tenacity, and resilience within the students by finding an area in which they are gifted. We want our students to have a positive self-concept. Students who do will take on challenges in areas they need to develop. We already possess a model of what this should look like in math, reading, and writing. If we expect to improve and strengthen a world where students have a strong work ethic and individual success, we need to create curriculums and times that are flexible to value all talents.

# Chapter 2
## The Toppling Dominoes and The Effect of Timing

(1)

I AM SURE THAT a school could never run the company FedEx. Change, especially in education, is extraordinarily tricky, and rapid development causes discomfort. Therefore, most auspicious shifts take years to be institutionalized. That is not necessarily a bad thing, but it has to be acknowledged as a limiting factor. Change scares people for a variety of reasons. Politicians do not want to scare voters. When politicians panic voters, they do not get reelected. So, the status quo is often the best wave to ride if an individual is in a position of power. How does a shift begin that changes mindsets and uses money responsibly to fund a system that fully nurtures people to be productive and successful citizens? The politicians need to develop a plan that allows them to not worry about what they value, which is voters.

Hypothetically, what if in education money was not a game changer, and a campaign to advertise the real benefits of the system laid out in chapter one was adopted universally? Political leaders are elected to make decisions with tax money. What if every local, state, and federal senator, congressperson, and the president agreed to make the developmental health of students their top priority? Would day-to-day actions and overriding philosophies change? Would it be possible to lure all people to invest in a system where the money is spent on developing the internal and external factors of child development? Change may not happen instantaneously, but decades later, the investment will likely outlive the people who initially put it in place and will inevitably have produced a positive result.

The Greek philosopher, Socrates, was born around 470 BC. He guided his students to answers through a series of questions, often encouraging them to draw their conclusions based on his questions. Socrates's doctrines were unique, and he was developing a western philosophical viewpoint at a time in history when it was in vogue to think creatively, philosophically, and with depth. Over two thousand years later, Plato's stories about Socrates are a cornerstone in most philosophy classes. What would Socrates say about successful change? He would teach us about change by encouraging us to define what truly matters.

Plato wrote that a young man, who looked up to Socrates, asked him, "What is the secret to success?"

Socrates told the young man to join him at a location along the river the following morning. The next morning came, and Socrates and the young man walked along the river together. Socrates diverted their stroll into the river. When the young man asked why they were doing this, Socrates replied, "You want to find out the secret to success, don't you?" As they wandered deeper and deeper into the water, the young man began to grow more and more skeptical.

Socrates was a large and powerful man. The two kept getting deeper and deeper into the river, and the young man questioned Socrates' motives. When the water got just about to the young man's neck, Socrates grabbed the young man's head, firmly grasped his hair, and drove the young man underwater. No matter how hard the young man struggled, Socrates kept the young man's head down. As much as the young man fought, he was not able to surface. The young man started turning blue and was approaching his last bits of consciousness. Just before he was about to breathe in the river water, Socrates pulled his head out of the water. The man was gasping for air. Holding his head firmly, Socrates asked the young man, "As you were struggling under the water, what did you want most?"

The young man replied, "Air."

Socrates responded, "When you want something as bad as a breath of air, you will find the secret to success."

The young man's need for air was immediate, and therefore the intensity of his desperation was concentrated. Many needs are not as apparent as air and often do not carry the same "in the moment" intensity. However, if a system is failing to satisfy the needs of the people, a constant desire as intense as wanting air needs to be universally pursued by all the stockholders. It is only then that growth will be made. For widespread transformation to occur, all decision makers need to feel like they are at the brink of their last breath to understand what they genuinely value. A series of deliberate and intentional decisions creates successful systems. Often, the underlying rationalizations for change are not visible, much like the concrete blocks of a basement that maintain the structure of a house. The house crumbles if those blocks are laid incorrectly;

the cement blocks are not visible, but they are vital to the stability of the dwelling. A solid wall is formed by putting one brick down carefully, followed by another. If a pattern of care and quality is observed, eventually there will be a solid wall.

Does change have to be done out of need, out of want, or by force? Can the framework for change be developed through the successes and failures of individuals and groups worldwide? The goal of any reform is to grow and progress for the benefit of all individuals and groups.

(2)

IN THE LATTER part of the 18th century, a horseback rider happened to come across a group of soldiers moving heavy logs. They were struggling with the weight of the wood and were not doing very well at achieving their task of clearing the road. The corporal who oversaw the men stood watching them struggle with the wood. Upon observing the scene, the passerby rider asked the corporal why he was not helping move the wood. The corporal asserted, "I am a corporal. My job is to give the orders." After a pause, the rider dismounted, talked to the men, and offered his help. The rider was tall and strong. With his help, the men were able to remove the wood and clear the path. Unknown to the corporal, the rider was General George Washington, the commander of the Federal troops.

After the wood was relocated, Washington did not criticize the corporal. He remounted his horse and said, "The next time your men need help, ask for the commander-in-chief." Washington was a man of action and often chose to speak through example. Years later, in a much more modern world, a similar experience would occur.

If a pin on a map was placed identifying one location where genius, innovation, willpower, and competition are in extensive stock, it would make sense for that pushpin to be tacked on Palo Alto, California, the home of Silicon Valley. This expanse of land is a hub for technological innovations and the advancements that have had a considerable impact on trends and styles, and it affects the way nearly all people manage their lives. Its development and growth followed a similar pattern to that of the United States. What happens in Silicon Valley affects the world; companies starting their account for one-third of the venture capital spent in the entire United States alone. The roots of Silicon Valley trace to Stanford University, and its influence has had an impact on the university's approach to educating its student body.

Fredrick Terman was the first Dean of Students of the College of Engineering at Stanford. He recognized the potential for widespread growth within the technology sector, so he highly encouraged Stanford students to stay local and start up their own companies. Terman perceived the increase of engineering students as an asset for the development of the west. What happened as a result? This area of the United States, which currently has about four million residents, produced the first integrated circuit, the first microcomputer, and the ARPANET, an early ancestor of the internet.

Once World War II ended, Stanford faced many demands. Soldiers were returning from the war, and the United States was heading into the prosperous baby boomer era. It was Fredrick Terman that suggested Stanford should lease lands to construct an office and technology park, known initially as Stanford Industrial Park. Stanford limited leases to innovative technology companies. So, not only was Stanford controlling the cutting edge of research technology, but they were setting up the ideal circumstances for a concentration of venture technology companies to settle there.

Hewlett-Packard is a prime example of one of the hundreds of companies that began in Stanford Industrial Park. Stanford graduates William Hewlett and David Packard, who started their company in a garage, would be one of the many companies that would move into Stanford Industrial Park. Stanford furthered their efforts by creating the Honors Cooperative Program. This program made it possible for full-time employees of the companies in the Stanford Industrial Park to pursue additional education at Stanford. It was like inviting a bunch of body builders to a protein shake convention. Stanford was getting a sneak peek at the innovations of some of the most exceptional programmers and engineers in the world, and those companies remained within walking distance from each other to cooperate and share ideas. Proximity also created a competitive environment, which further increased the rate of productivity.

Corporate giants such as Eastman Kodak, General Electric, and Lockheed were tenants alongside Hewlett-Packard, and naturally, they sent their employees to Stanford. With all this talent in one area, law firms began popping up everywhere offering services to protect the patents that were needed with each new advancement. One of the most famous inventions was the Shockley Semiconductor, in which William Shockley used silicon for making transistors. Shockley worked with other innovators such as Robert Noyce and Gordon Moore, who would continue their work and eventually establish Intel, which has designed more microprocessors than any other company in history.

When General George Washington dismounted his horse to help Federal soldiers, he was setting an example of how great leaders conduct themselves. He was a reliable decision maker and a visionary. Washington understood the value of the blue-collar example, especially in the British colonies where leadership would be vital in the face of British oppression. He recognized that his standard would have a considerable effect on the people around him. Both George Washington and Frederick Terman had a vision. Progress is made in business and education during a revolution in a very similar way. Clear and direct guidance through insight sets an example and executes the vision with purpose.

In 1854, George Eastman was born on a 10-acre farm in Waterville, New York. He was principally self-educated. The family moved to Rochester, New York, a city snowballing in business because of its rapid advancements in industrialization. At the age of eight, Eastman's father would die, and to survive, his mother took in boarders. The money she made ensured George would be able to continue to go to school. She was a staunch believer in education and worked vigorously to make sure young George Eastman went to school.

Further challenges struck when George's sister died of polio.

This proved to be too much financial stress on the family, and George had to stop attending school to help support the household. From the start, Eastman had the odds stacked against him. As a messenger boy for an insurance firm, Eastman received three dollars per week. At an early age he showed an interest in gadgets and spent evenings teaching himself accounting skills to advance to a higher paying job. It paid off. In 1874, Eastman was appointed to be a junior clerk at Rochester Savings Bank, and his weekly salary increased to fifteen dollars per week.

With Eastman's newfound income, he purchased a wet plate camera and the various equipment used by this type of camera. It is a common misconception that George Eastman invented photography. Ten years before Eastman's purchase, President Abraham Lincoln would become the first American President ever to be photographed. The actual pioneer of photography was the French inventor, Nicéphore Niépce. However, he never mass produced his device, so Eastman is associated with the advent of photography.

In 1878, George Eastman planned to take an expedition to Santo Domingo and wanted to chronicle the journey utilizing photography. Eastman described the equipment size as "a packhorse load." He did not end up making the trip to Santo Domingo because he became fixated with the concept of the camera. During the day, Eastman worked at the bank, but at night he was obsessed with trying to create a dry plate that was light sensitive. This was all being done in his mother's kitchen. A dry plate would relieve the photographer of the overwhelming amount of chemicals that were needed for wet plate photography. Some nights Eastman exerted himself to the point that he would fall asleep on the kitchen floor.

After three years of experimenting, Eastman had created a formula that effectively captured images with a dry plate. He also developed a machine that could mass produce dry plates. Eastman knew that the number of photographers in the world was increasing rapidly, and he recognized that if he could mass produce the plates, he would most likely have a profitable company. He bought a two-horsepower motor and founded the Eastman Kodak Company. At one point early in the company's production of plates, Eastman almost faced ruin when he produced and sold an extensive series of plates that did not work. He replaced them without question stating, "Making good on those plates took our last dollar, but what we had left was more important: our reputation." A strong reputation and calculated moves allowed for survival during challenging times.

George Eastman bet that interest in photography would continue to expand rapidly, and he recognized the potential that the everyday consumers possessed. In 1885, George Eastman began selling a new invention: roll film. It initially flopped. Photographers who were used to glass slides did not buy into this new development. His idea could have stopped there. Instead, in 1888, he reached out to the general public with a camera called the Brownie, named for its brown and rectangular look. He advertised: "You press the button, and we do the rest." George Eastman had a vision, and he was willing to work for nothing on the project in his mother's kitchen to attain a high level of success.

Eastman involved himself in all aspects of the company. Initially, Eastman held a tight grip on his vision, micromanaging his startup down to the last detail. The iconic red and yellow color combination, the logo, and the sales of the company all came from its visionary leader. Eastman even chose the company name—with no origin—because he felt that "K" was a strong letter. He was not hesitant to walk through the trenches of his workplace.

The turning point for Kodak, the Brownie camera, would allow people to capture and photograph moments in their lives. Mass production began in the early 1900s. The Brownie initially sold for $1.00, and it introduced the snapshot to the masses. The gadget was a basic point and shoot box camera developed and marketed to generate sales of Kodak roll films. Because of how easy it was to use, coupled with its low cost, the Brownie camera exceeded all sales expectations. Eastman's vision resulted in the advancement of one of the most profitable companies of the first half of the 20th century. Photography became the next advancement to record human and natural history. The United States relied on these advancements and innovations during the Second World War. They arose directly from Kodak. At one point, Kodak was one of the largest consumers of silver in the world because of its use when creating film.

In 2012, Kodak filed for bankruptcy. Over a century had passed. At the end of 2011, Kodak stock fell to an all-time low of 54 cents per share. What befell this giant? In 1976, Kodak's researchers had invented the digital camera. However, Kodak was a corporation that had raked in profits on consumables for years. Film, chemicals, and photo paper were the lifeblood of the company. The leadership was locked into these products. The concept of a camera without consumables was not within the vision of the company's direction. Hence, Kodak, the inventor of the digital camera, was behind the eight ball when the digital camera revolution began. Incredibly, Kodak held the patents on digital imaging and processing techniques. In 1986, they had created the first megapixel sensor. Still, the company would not shift away from film, even though a change in consumer interest was apparent by the way people were using technology. The company paid the price with a catastrophic collapse. Similarly, the American automotive sector would make comparable mistakes in the 1970s and 1980s with the production of large, gas guzzling cars. These corporations failed to see the progress that Volkswagen, Toyota, Honda, and many other foreign car companies were making with fuel efficiency. As fuel prices increased, fuel efficient car companies were ready.

Increased success has a direct link to the ability to adapt at the right time and visionaries who are able to make difficult decisions. When proposals are made to change deep-rooted practices, it is very natural to balk. If organizations lack the vision to see how they will need to evolve to continue to be competitive and successful, then an increase in frustration, confusion, and collapse result. Kodak's decisions parallel the corporal who just watched his troops work. When business as usual was used, people failed to see needed tweaks and shifts. Washington saw the situation for what it was and adjusted his leadership to what was needed. Success does not just happen. Demands must be filled and needs and trends are always changing. If the corporal had the vision, he would have acted outside the realm of his expected character, but his actions would have been just what his men needed. In the case of Kodak, seizing the shift from consumable cameras to digital photography most likely would have caused the company to flourish.

During the 1970s and 80s, the management of Kodak was grounded in tradition and playing the safe poker hand. For over a century, starting in 1888, the fundamental principles of dry film photography did not change. Management followed the pattern of what had historically worked. However, the executives failed to visit the vast trenches as Eastman had. The world does evolve, and innovations cause constant change. Kodak did not develop with the changes in technology. The longer a leader spends time in the hollows of their work, the greater the possibility that the leader will have their finger on the pulse, ultimately affecting timely decisions. Leaders who have their eyes on progress and not entirely on the bottom line create an environment for potential success. These visionaries see trends in society and make consumer-based decisions. George Eastman also had one key component that most successful individuals have: humble roots that had to grow on their own.

Being a visionary does not guarantee success, but the odds of success go up if significant investments are made in development. Some engineers at Kodak recognized the goldmine on which they were sitting. They produced the first digital camera. Executives, like the corporal, did not work with the troops, and because of this, the disconnect caused failure.

(3)
*Where there is no vision, the people perish, but he that keepeth the law, happy is he.*
Proverbs 29:18

JEFF JORGENSEN'S MODEST beginnings are a stark contrast to his net worth. As of 2019, Forbes Magazine assessed Jorgensen's net value at well over 155 billion US dollars. Jorgensen was born in 1964 to a teenage mother who stayed married to his father for a little under a year. He lived on an Albuquerque, New Mexico ranch, which was occupied for generations by his family. His family would move to Houston when he was young. In the summer, a young Jeff would return to the ranch where he started his life to support his grandfather by performing jobs such as fixing windmills and vaccinating cattle. He was adopted by a Cuban immigrant who married his mother, and his last name was changed to Bezos.

There was something extraordinary about young Jeff. As a toddler, he systematically tried to disassemble his crib, and as a young teen, he would construct electrical gadgets around the house, one of which was an alarm to prevent his siblings from entering his room. As he grew older, Bezos continued to display a strong aptitude for mechanical and electrical objects. Bezos would become the valedictorian of his high school class, which led him to Princeton University. He would originally study engineering, but quickly realized his passion for computer science and specialized in electrical engineering.

Jeff Bezos was bright. He was elected to the Phi Beta Kappa and

Tau Beta Pi engineering societies. Bezos was a skilled engineer, but employment circumstances led him to Wall Street. He stuck close to trading in the computer science sector. In the infancy of computer networks, Bezos worked for an international trade company named Fital. He helped Fital build a trade network and performed similar work at Bankers Trust and D.E. Shaw and Company. Bezos recognized two opportunities that were developing. First, he saw that the use of electronic network systems was expanding at an exponential rate. The internet was changing the way consumers behaved and communicated. Second, he knew that under a recent interpretation of the law, the Supreme Court ruled online retailers would not have to collect sales tax in states where they were not physically present. Not charging a sales tax would put any online retailer at a considerable advantage. Bezos had a vision. He put together the formula for a tax-free network and business model on a cross country trek from New York to Seattle and outlined the fundamental structure of the internet Godzilla, Amazon.com. This supergiant accounted for over 232 billion dollars in online sales in 2018. Jeff Bezos personally chose the company name with the realization in the early stages of the internet that in an online search, the word "Amazon," which begins with an "A," would come up first on an alphabetical list. This was a simple tactic, but so was the action of George Washington hopping down off his horse to help soldiers and George Eastman's belief that the letter "K" had value. Small actions can have lasting impacts.

Bezos had other insights. He realized that there was a worldwide demand for books, which had a low price point. He debated initially on peddling CDs, software, computer hardware, and videos online. He saw that the demand for books would help his startup be a success and bet correctly. As the company developed, Amazon.com added broad variety to their product lines. Bezos had his hand in almost every aspect of the company. When a lot of the internet market was fast moving, Bezos decided to grow his website slowly. This meant that Amazon, unlike many of its contemporaries, was not artificially inflated. When the internet market burst in the earliest part of the 21st century, Bezos's highly criticized slow-moving business model provided stability.

What would have happened if Jeff Bezos was the CEO of Eastman Kodak during the 1970s, 80s, and 90s? Hypothetically, Jeff Bezos would have etched out a different path for the film giant. Bezos was an engineer and computer scientist. The role of corporate leaders is to provide vision and direction for a company, and leadership is supposed to evolve as the company grows by investing their time and direction on visionary moves. In 1976, Kodak owned 90% of the global share of the film market, and at the time possessed the first digital camera. They decided not to market it. Would Jeff Bezos have made the same decisions? In 1994, Apple would pioneer a camera called the QuickTake. The QuickTake would display the Apple label but was manufactured by Kodak. Without the Kodak name on the label, the company would never gain momentum in the digital camera market, which catalyzed a chain of events leading to one of the most significant corporate collapses in American history.

The business models of Kodak and Amazon are starkly different. Their strategies parallel a game of poker. On one hand, Kodak leadership holds three-of-a-kind, a decent hand, and one that will hold up on most rounds. Meanwhile, Jeff Bezos possesses two of a kind, which will not beat three-of-a-kind, but he has a plan. He bluffs. Bezos is crafty. He knows that all hands are beatable if he can get his opponent on unstable ground. In the case of Kodak, the eroded soil was their unwavering commitment to stick with conventional film production. Film had lasted for nearly a century, but digital photography was the future. Bezos had a vision into the future, and Kodak was locked in on the moment, fixated on the bottom line. It failed to shift for advancement. When faced with adversity, Bezos bet wisely. In the early 1990s, film was alive and well. Instead of betting on the future, Kodak leadership folded with three-of-a-kind because they did not want to venture their pot of money on a nearly all-in bet on digital photography. Unfortunately, a series of folded hands cost Rochester, New York a company and let them bear witness to the deterioration of a significant corporate label.

In his interview, Sal Khan talked at length about an enrichment room he was put in at an early age. As a second grader, he had to make decisions about what he was going to do and how he was going to do it. That environment guided his development. When people practice decision making, difficult decisions become easier to make.

In 23 BC, the Roman poet Horace wrote in his book, *The Odes*, "Carpe diem", meaning, "Seize the day." Typically, Horace is not fully quoted. The full quote from *The Odes* is "Carpe diem, quam minimum credula postero", which when translated into English means, "Seize the present; trust tomorrow as little as you may." Carpe diem has guided sports teams, warriors, and companies. The second portion of the quote has fallen through the cracks. It points to a much deeper meaning that Horace was trying to convey: there needs to be a balance between the speed of progress and responsible decision making. The process and the product need to be wed together yet watched independently. Exceptional leaders understand this.

(4)

A YOUNG BOY born in rags grows into riches after pursuing entrepreneurship in an industry that was on the cusp of booming. This is the American dream. Andrew Carnegie's narrative is similar to that of George Eastman. In the case of Eastman, success hinged on photography. Jeff Bezos took advantage of the rapid growth of internet opportunities as a sales market, and in the case of Andrew Carnegie, wealth was accumulated through an understanding that steel would constitute the foundation for the American Industrial Revolution. Vision plus opportunity produces increased potential for success. A young life of privilege does not guarantee success. However, is there a moral obligation that comes with accomplishment? When a person or group becomes successful, what is the next course of action? What if the poker game goes so well that now the pot of money is more than any person would ever need? Then what? What obligation, if any, does a wealthy individual have to society? What moral responsibility, if any, comes with success?

In 1835, Andrew Carnegie was born in Dunfermline, Scotland. He was brought up in a weaver's cottage, in which the main room served as both the dining room and the sleeping quarters. The life of a weaver paid poorly, and his family was on the brink of starvation. With a loan, Carnegie's father moved his family to the United States. They settled in the town of Allegheny, Pennsylvania. As poor children did in the 1840s, young Carnegie went to work as a bobbin boy working 72-hour weeks for $1.20. Bobbin boys often worked shoeless, climbing on fast-moving textile bobbin machines. It was a dangerous job in which many children lost toes, fingers, or even became permanently crippled.

As Carnegie approached his 18th birthday, he began to work for the Pennsylvania Railroad Company for $4.00 per week. Thomas Scott mentored him. At the time, Scott was a station agent. He would later go on to become the fourth president of the Pennsylvania Railroad, the United States Assistant Secretary of War during the American Civil War, and worked on part of the Compromise of 1877 in which federal troops were removed from the south as part of the reconstruction efforts following the Civil War. Carnegie and Scott, two very talented men with incredibly bright futures, were working together. Imagine the odds!

Scott taught Carnegie about management and cost control. This knowledge would serve Carnegie well, and as Scott advanced in the ranks, he brought Carnegie along with him. It was through Scott that Carnegie would begin a relationship with J. Edgar Thompson, the first president of the Pennsylvania Railroad. During the Civil War, Carnegie oversaw railway transportation to

Washington, D.C. After the Battle of Bull Run, he personally supervised the repair of the rail and telegraph systems, which helped the Union forces gain momentum. Like George Washington, Jeff Bezos, and George Eastman, Carnegie learned from the ground up. Carnegie understood the value of oil, and in 1864 bought a $40,000 farm in Venango County, Pennsylvania that would yield over $1,000,000 in oil. Carnegie also recognized that wartime production caused a significant increase in the demand for iron and steel. Steel was costly to make, so initially, Carnegie took advantage of the need for iron and continued to profit. He had a vision.

After the Civil War, Carnegie left the railroads to devote all his energies on the iron trades. With his close connections to Thompson and Scott, Carnegie was able to acquire the Keystone Bridge Company. Carnegie named his first manufacturing plant after Thompson, and naturally his largest customer was the Pennsylvania Railroad. Once Carnegie acted on his vision to transition to steel production via the Bessemer converter, his legacy was set. His pattern was clear: vision, change, and progress. It was a pattern that would continue throughout his lifetime.

Soon, Carnegie was one of the most affluent men in the world. His upbringing and experiences would continue to have a strong influence on his vision after he became extraordinarily wealthy. But, just how wealthy was Carnegie? In 2019 US dollars, Carnegie's net worth would be nearly 310 billion dollars. However, in 1919 Carnegie would die at the age of 83 with only 10% of his value from his wealthiest years. One may assume that poor decision making, lack of vision, and ignorance of the changes in the world would lead to Carnegie's financial change, when in fact that is far from the truth. It was Carnegie's vision that purposefully continued to guide him.

What obligation does a successful entrepreneur have to society? Carnegie believed that serving others was an obligation of a successful person. The fortune that Carnegie accumulated was not merely given away. The same grass-roots leadership and vision that caused Carnegie's success in the first place guided his philanthropy. Andrew Carnegie was poor as a child, so he understood the disadvantages of poverty and, in turn, recognized the advantages of being independently wealthy.

(5)

SIR HUMPHREY CHETHAM was born in 1580 in Crumpsall, Lancashire, England. The members of Chetham's family enjoyed lives of affluence and privilege. Unlike Carnegie, Eastman, and Bezos, Chetham did not have to formulate a vision to become prosperous due to his wealthy birthright. In his early adult years, he began to trade in textiles. He realized that the price of textiles was higher in Manchester than in London. He profited from this knowledge, which allowed him to acquire real estate. Chetham was born into prosperity, and he possessed a vision. His success reached the ears of the British hierarchy, and in 1631, he was invited to be knighted. He refused. With a distinction as a knight, Chetham feared that the British Parliament would possess his wealth upon his death, and therefore he protected his assets.

How did Chetham guard his money? He donated it to form a

bluecoat school for poor boys. These were English schools in parishes, erected to educate the poor about literacy, writing, and the mastery of essential trades. This school later became the hospital in Manchester, and eventually the building was converted into the Chetham School of Music. Upon Chetham's death in 1653, it was disclosed that he had bequeathed money to start a library. The library in Manchester was the first public library in which all people could view books. Until Chetham's library was built, the poor citizens of England had no access to public books. Years later, socialists Karl Marx and Friedrich Engels would regularly read and meet in the Chetham library.

Two hundred years later across the Atlantic, the land of the free was not exactly equitable for all people. A country founded on the grit of the common man—the nation that refused a monarch and was the melting pot of the world—did not possess a single free and public library.

The United States was young, and there were leftover practices from Colonial America. A 1647 Massachusetts law mandated that every town of 50 or more families support a school and every town of 100 or more families support a Latin or grammar school where a few boys could learn Latin in preparation for college, the ministry, or law. Seventy percent of colonists in the Middle New England Colonies were literate compared to 40 percent of their counterparts in England. In practice, virtually all New England towns tried to provide some schooling for their children. Boys and girls attended the elementary schools. They learned to read, write, cipher, and studied religion. Farms dominated the south. There was a low population density, and only very basic of skills were needed for labor. Therefore, education was generally reserved for the rich, and in many cases, privatized. Many white children of a lower economic class as well as nearly all black children went unschooled. Literacy rates were significantly lower in the south than the north; this remained true until the late nineteenth century.

Subscription libraries were limited to a select few. Subscription libraries were precisely what their name indicates: members only. The only exception to the rule of the "subscription" was when the patron was a student. Education in the United States was greatly improved during the early 1800s, but it was slow moving. In 1839, the country's first public normal school was founded by the Secretary of the Massachusetts Board of Education, Horace Mann. In 1852, Massachusetts became the first state to require all children to go to school. However, the poor and uneducated were still not allowed in libraries.

The implications of such a system gave a definite and clear advantage to people of wealth. The rich continued to have educational benefits using the library, while the poor did not have access to books. Literacy is critical for those who are poor or oppressed to unlock their potential and improve their lives. The inability to go into a library did not allow those who lacked resources the opportunity to expand their minds. What changed? The answer comes in the form of Andrew Carnegie, whose contribution to libraries would become almost as significant as the Gutenberg printing press.

If scaling the mountain is the route to success, charity is the equivalent of reaching for the clouds. In 1901, Andrew Carnegie was 66 years old and considering retirement. He had spent a lifetime creating one of the most profitable companies in United States history, the United States Steel Corporation. Through a corporate takeover sale, Carnegie made a profit of $225,639,000. In 2014, this would amount to nearly 13.6 billion US dollars. The actual company was valued at 1.4 billion dollars, which equaled 4% of the entire United States economy. This was a colossal acquisition.

A visionary to the core, Carnegie wondered: what now? There was no way for one man or one family to spend or need this enormous sum of money, and Carnegie knew this. When Carnegie sold his company, he was paid in 50-year gold bonds. He had a special vault built in New Jersey, where he locked up the bonds and refused to look at them ever again out of fear that his fortune would vanish.

Once a visionary, always a visionary. To imagine the future, a person needs to appreciate the past. Carnegie did. He knew what it was like to be less privileged. The next phase of Andrew Carnegie's life was devoted to philanthropy. Upon his retirement, Carnegie proclaimed, "I promise to take an income no more than $50,000 per annum! Beyond this I need ever earn, make no effort to increase my fortune, but spend the surplus on benevolent purposes." He practiced a lifestyle of personal moderation. Though incredible, Carnegie's story is not complicated. A powerful businessperson can turn his attention toward the public to do good for the people from whom he became rich.

What were Carnegie's projects? First and foremost, Carnegie

was a scholar. He was an avid reader and made many claims that his retirement would be a blessing because he could devote more time to reading scholarly works. More importantly, Carnegie believed in literacy for all people, no matter how poor or rich. Early on his philanthropy focused his attention on spelling reform. This was long before he retired. For most people living in the United States before the turn of the 20th century, it was acceptable to spell incorrectly as long as the written message was clear. A classic example of this practice can be seen in the handwritten journals of Lewis and Clark. When reading the journals, one can see that they are not only riddled with misspellings, but also that some words are spelled in multiple ways on the same page. These were men whose families cavorted with presidents, yet they did not spell correctly. Carnegie was vocal about a need for spelling reform. Consistent with his effort to further education, Andrew Carnegie's most notable interest was the establishment of a free public library system throughout the United States.

Enoch Pratt was a wealthy philanthropist in Baltimore, Maryland. He amassed most of his wealth in the mercantile trade but also had various other business ventures. In the middle of his life, Pratt was inspired by a more notable name, George Peabody. Peabody was the richest man living in the United States before the Civil War. Peabody began his career importing dry goods from England, and later, cotton. As time went on, he grossed a massive fortune in merchant banking. It would be Peabody that would take Junius Morgan (the father of J.P. Morgan) as a partner in 1854. Like Carnegie, Peabody was born to a frugal family with seven siblings. As a result, when he reached the pinnacle of fortune, he turned to philanthropy. He remembered what it was like to be poor and felt a sense of obligation to those who faced similar circumstances.

Successful people often affect each other because they share the same experiences of grit and determination. George Peabody established the Peabody Education Fund to develop schools to improve the lives of impoverished students in the south. He did similar works of charity in London and created many public libraries throughout the New England states that stretched into the south. It was Peabody's generosity that inspired Enoch Pratt to finance building of the Pratt Free Library in Baltimore, Maryland. Pratt and Carnegie's paths crossed through business, and in the 1890s, Andrew Carnegie visited Enoch Pratt. While there, Carnegie spent time investigating the library that Pratt had established, visiting with both staff and patrons. The visit had a significant impact on him, so much so that years later Carnegie would credit Pratt as "[his] guide and inspiration." The idea of a free and public library system, open to all people, was handed down from Peabody to Pratt, and then to Carnegie. Though it seems that the philanthropic stars aligned, this was no accidental association. A method of mentorship existed. Greatness does attract greatness, and similarly, charity promotes further charity.

Starting in 1883, Andrew Carnegie was responsible for funding the construction of 2,509 Carnegie libraries. Most were built in the United States, but there were 660 erected in England and Ireland, 125 in Canada, and others were constructed in New Zealand and Australia. Almost every library built with Andrew Carnegie's money was constructed through a contract guided by the "Carnegie Formula." This formula considered the town or city's commitment to not only building the library but also their ability to sustain it. The town was obligated to demonstrate the need for a public library, provide a building site, provide ten percent of the cost of the library's construction, and support its future operation. However, the most important condition was that the library must provide free service for all people. Though the building style and location were generally left up to the community, nearly all Carnegie libraries were built with two distinct features that were requested by Andrew Carnegie himself. First, a Carnegie funded library usually had a large stack of stairs leading up to the front door to symbolize a person growing in knowledge. The second recognizable feature was a simple lamppost out in front of the library, representing enlightenment. Most Carnegie libraries also were constructed with a fireplace, an odd pairing with combustible paper books. Many early libraries were heated by coal furnaces.

In order to ensure that the library would be financed long after it had been built, residents of each town had to agree to pay taxes to fund all potential costs. Carnegie was passing along his good fortune by empowering others. Municipalities had to share in the investment to ensure they valued what they were getting.

The vision did not stop there. Carnegie also had to try and change the way that people viewed libraries—and the way that library staff viewed the population at large. Initially, the common practice of service at a library was for the patron to go to a desk, fill out a request form, and present it to the reference librarian who would fetch the book from the stacks. Often librarians would simply decide whether they trusted someone based on outward appearance; indeed, there were moments when a poor person was denied access to a book simply because of their status.

A single reference librarian retrieving a requested book was a time-consuming task, and it often became an act of cultural or economic discrimination. Carnegie recognized this. Carnegie's architects designed a new system in which the stacks of books were put on shelves accessible to the patrons. Without a librarian making judgments on who should or should not be trusted with books, citizens from all walks of life were able to access everything that the library had to offer. One librarian would be assigned to oversee the entire operation. This original design was experimented with for the first time in Carnegie's backyard of Pittsburgh, Pennsylvania.

In 1969, a study administered by Dr. George Bobinkski of the State University of Buffalo revealed that 1,554 of the original 1,681 Carnegie libraries were still standing structures, with 911 still actively used as libraries. This study was done eighty years after the first Carnegie library was built. The number of patrons over those eighty years was in the billions, making the contribution of the free and public library system immeasurable. The improved educational opportunities for impoverished people from the United States and abroad can be credited, at least in part, to Carnegie's vision. Was Carnegie special? Absolutely. Was he unique? Absolutely not. Carnegie was a disciple of George Peabody, who most regard as the first modern philanthropist. Peabody influenced generations of philanthropists, most notably Johns Hopkins, John D. Rockefeller, and Bill Gates. Their contributions have exceeded many billions of dollars. Most colleges send out quarterly magazines and list their donors. To some degree, all donors are philanthropists influenced by the decision of so many before them to give back to the society that helped them reach financial elevation.

Nearly all of George Eastman's commercial estate was donated to the University of Rochester and the Massachusetts Institute of Technology. His fortune helped found the Eastman School of Music, a globally recognized musical institution. Most of Eastman's donations were made using the alias, Mr. Smith.

Jeff Bezos turned 55 in 2019. He is a youngster in the world of philanthropy, but like his predecessors, he has maintained a strong corporate vision. He is far from retired. In 2013, Jeff Bezos purchased the Washington Post in a 250-million-dollar cash deal. In 2009, he was named Time Magazine's Person of the Year and in 2012, Fortune Magazine identified Bezos as Businessperson of the Year. Jeff Bezos has been highly criticized for not giving enough to charity, especially in Seattle, Washington where he resides. If comparisons are made between Bezos, Eastman, and Carnegie, his critics are right. However, he is in his 50s. Time will tell whether he will follow in the footsteps of his predecessors. Considering his profitable string of visionary decisions, it seems likely that he will carve out his own version of philanthropy.

Thus far, the Bezos Family Foundation has been set up to foster better learning environments and support young leaders. Jeff and his former wife, MacKenzie, donated large sums of money to fund research toward the fight against many forms of cancer, and a significant donation was made to Princeton University, their alma mater. In 2013, Jeff Bezos was quoted as saying, "Giving away money takes as much attention as building a successful company." Carnegie's actions echo this sentiment. Though generosity seems easy, perhaps Jeff Bezos is right; philanthropy takes vision, and it was a vision that got him to a place to have the opportunity to give back.

Philanthropy does equate to sainthood. There has been criticism that has been directed at Jeff Bezos, including his treatment towards the homeless, minimum wage, and the restrictions of workers at Amazon warehouses. This does not invalidate his generosity toward specific causes, but it does acknowledge that the extremely wealthy may not always see themselves as having an obligation to give back to society as a whole—only certain parts of it. In Bezos's case, he chose to support cancer research. Carnegie too, had specific areas of interest he chose to focus his charitable interests on. There is no obligation for a wealthy person to give to others. Gifting money can paint a target on the philanthropist. There is no defined percentage of philanthropy or obligation of service that comes with wealth. However, service to others is a self-evident truth, and whether a person is worth billions of dollars or is penniless, every single person can be philanthropic in one way or another. Philanthropy means the love of humanity. Philanthropy relates to the private initiatives for the public good, focusing on quality of life for all people. Ask yourself this: what are you wealthy in? Once you have defined this, ask yourself: are you a philanthropist with your wealth?

# Interview with Nicole Dreiske
*November 2, 2018*
*New York, New York*

I met Nicole Dreiske while I was presenting at a conference on parenting in New York City. Dreiske is the Executive Director of the International Children's Media Center in Chicago, Illinois. Dreiske's work is devoted to educating children on how to prepare their minds before they start watching screens. She focuses her efforts on teaching young children to be aware of the content they are consuming on electronic screens and how they are affected by it.

**Albrecht:** Who am I here with?
**Dreiske:** Nicole Dreiske. I am the Executive Director of the International Children's Media Center, and the author of *The Upside of Digital Devices- How to Make Your Child More Screen Smart, Literate and Emotionally Intelligent.*
**Albrecht:** And where do you live?
**Dreiske:** I live in Chicago.
**Albrecht:** And how old are you?
**Dreiske:** I'm sixty-six.
**Albrecht:** So, here's my question. I'd like you to think over sixty-six years. Who is your favorite educator or teacher?
**Dreiske:** This is so easy to answer; Ms. Bush, my junior year English teacher. I became an English teacher because of her. Up until

then, I would have to say my experiences in school were all about mitigating self-perceived failures. I could never get to a level that I thought was as good as I wanted to be. And, what happened with Ms. Bush is something that happened back in the classroom. So, there were four levels of learning. The second level is the national average, third level is a little above. They put us in tracks. I was in fourth level English.

**Albrecht:** So, the fourth level would be your most challenging?

**Dreiske:** Yes, fourth level would be your most challenging. So, relatively speaking, fourth level kids were the ones who at least tuned in and wanted to achieve something academically. So, she gave us all Cs on our first papers, and none of us had ever gotten a C before in our whole life. This was this huge wakeup call, that OH MY GOODNESS, I am not going to be able to brownnose my way through this. I'm not going to be able to find out what she wants and play to her particular perspective of what I should be learning. I'm going to have to fall back on my own resources, and what I love about that experience is as soon as I broke that mold, I realized that all the self-blame, the self-incrimination of what I wasn't achieving in school was coming because I was trying to fit myself into a box. I had identified the patterns that box wanted me to emulate. What I became really great at was breaking the pattern and forming a new one that would take me farther than ever before. When I got from Ms. Bush on a paper about Moby Dick "A+, write a sequel," was the happiest day of my life. I became an English major and went through the rest of my academic life with tremendous confidence. It was a breakthrough for me.

**Albrecht:** What school was Ms. Bush at?

**Dreiske:** She was at New Trier, which back in the day was considered one of the top three in the country. New Trier is in Winnetka, which is a suburb of Chicago. It was a very interesting social place.

**Albrecht:** So, back to Ms. Bush. What are three words to describe her?

**Dreiske:** Passionate about learning. Rigorous. Committed to the best potential of every student.

## Reflection:

Teachers create pivotal moments in students' lives, whether those moments are of joy or sorrow. I have attended the funerals of many grandparents, some parents, and even pets. I have also been there for the joyful moments on a sports field, at dance recitals, and during scout ceremonies. The students I teach are not my children, but I feel like I spend as much time with them as my three biological children. The closeness of a classroom makes drawing hard lines with students challenging, but necessary.

Nicole Dreiske's teacher understood that there are two curriculums. There is the prescribed curriculum, where students must master a set of skills that the teacher wants the students to have, which Dreiske called "fitting into a box." Most students want to succeed and please both their family and their teachers. Attaining solid grades is part of this desire. But what, exactly, is a grade? Some grades are created by a teacher's feelings about how well a student has mastered a skill; others are generated by data that indicates what the student has mastered.

The second set of laurels that Dreiske referred to has to come from the student. Ms. Bush was not just giving her students the tools they would need to survive in the real world, but also building a classroom mentality and environment where students had to develop their direction through self-reliance. Ms. Bush did this in the harshest way possible for high-achieving students: she gave them grades that were far below the standard they were used to. Ms. Bush immediately took every one of her students out of their comfort zone by putting the obligation of learning onto her students.

Should schools teach failure? Getting a C felt like defeat to Dreiske; she referred to a lower grade as a "wakeup call." Is going to school all about the attainment of distinguished grades? A school is supposed to prepare students to be ready for life. However, most schools' mission statements focus on developing students to be career and college ready, without any discussion of other forms of success. We need people to exit high school ready to be productive citizens, and productivity does not always come in the form of a career or college.

Many schools are determined to get their students career and college ready, but if a school has not taught a student how to be resilient in the face of collapse, how will that student respond the first time they make a critical mistake at work or in college? There is even a broader issue. Top colleges look at a student's grades and extracurricular activities for admission to their institution. If a student falls below standard on an assignment or assessment but is shown how to be resilient, they may graduate with a lower grade point average. If a student receives high marks but is never challenged, he or she goes off to a prestigious college where they most likely will face some hurdle in the classroom or with the people they live with. They may not be prepared to deal with this. The trouble is that the system of grading students based on a product, not a process, creates a flawed system that does not adequately prepare students for adversity.

I teach fourth grade in New York State. Every spring in grades three through eight is state testing season. There have always been tests to assess student achievement, but at the turn of the millennium, high stakes testing began to come into play. Testing has been around for centuries; colonists brought the practice of testing from Europe when they developed schools in the newly formed United States. Testing was never used to evaluate the teachers' or schools' effectiveness, and students who failed were deemed to be incapable of learning and therefore were subsequently left behind. Slowly, this mindset has shifted.

In 2001, the United States Congress passed the No Child Left Behind Act (NCLB). This was a turning point in testing. Under this legislation, states were held economically hostage. Title I funding provided federal dollars to states where students have been deemed disadvantaged. For states to continue to receive Title I funding, they had to comply with NCLB regulations; those states that refused received considerably less funding than their compliant counterparts. States had to assess students at chosen grade levels to prove that their schools were making adequate yearly progress, or AYP. Schools failing to make AYP for two consecutive years were deemed "In Need of Improvement," and they were required to follow guidelines to develop an improvement plan. For schools under an improvement plan, students had the option to transfer to a "better" school within the school district.

When testing first was introduced, the consequences of the scores fell on the student. This has entirely changed. Now, when students do not make growth, they get labeled, but it is the school that needs to come up with the plan. The blame has shifted, and community trends are ignored.

Nicole Dreiske's teacher, Ms. Bush, was not afraid of the system. She stood firm with the understanding that her students would have to pass and, more importantly, become self-reliant to be successful in life. Dreiske identified two things Ms. Bush did early in the year. First, she shifted the responsibility of learning back onto the students; second, she was not scared to teach students how to handle failure. The fallout of high stakes testing has created a system in which panic takes over when students fail, even at the primary grades. If students are pushed hard academically and have an understanding that they must pass or meet the standard, fear of failure sets in. I see it firsthand.

Our state currently does not have a time limit for the test. The result is that those students who are afraid to fail will sit in a chair for over five hours, meticulously looking over their work to ensure that they succeed at the highest level. A nine-year-old should never have this experience. That fear of failure leads to compliance. Students do what Dreiske said: "fit [themselves] in a box." If the system delivers a set curriculum, and students are persistent and compliant, they graduate. There is no prerequisite to demonstrate a proficiency in resiliency to graduate. This is like talking about swimming, watching movies about how to swim, and writing out the sequence of movements of how to swim—without ever getting into the water. If you can do all that, you know what it takes to swim. However, unless a student gets in the water, do they really know how to swim? We are essentially letting our students drown under a system that does not have a period in a child's education where failure is not penalized.

Dreiske's interview proves that when a teacher puts the onus of learning on the student in a safe environment, lifelong learning occurs. Students will fail at times, but they will also learn how to face and overcome that failure, and in doing so will learn resilience. If grades matter so much in high school that it will affect the entrance to college, then the place to learn lessons about resiliency is not at the secondary level. Resilience in the face of disappointment needs to be a cornerstone of elementary education. However, if testing mandates remain at the primary level, fear of failure will continue to dominate the classroom.

Thank you, Ms. Bush, for having the guts to do right by your students.

## Chapter 3
## Glenn Cunningham: The Underestimation of Soft Skills

(1)

THE COMFORTING AROMA of sweet tea lingers in the air as you secure your selection from a variety of fresh scones in the pastry display case. The line in the London tearoom is ten people deep. Casually glancing at the other people in line, you recognize the singer and songwriter, Paul McCartney. He is standing in front of you. You know him and his legacy. He was a Beatle! Will you say hello? Moreover, if you do, what would you discuss? There is a bizarre human response when meeting an iconic person. Their humanness is no different from anyone else's, but since recognizable people happen to be more visible and talked about, there is a sense of awe when being in their presence. Whether you are meeting Paul McCartney or saying hello to a coworker, you are depending on your soft skills. If you are fortunate enough to know a bit about the person beforehand, it will be much easier to strike up a conversation with Paul McCartney.

Alberto Perez was born in Cali, Colombia. Like so many innovators, his life did not start smoothly. He was raised by a single mother who had to manage three jobs to support her family. Alberto's passion was dancing, and though he could not afford lessons, he won Colombia's national lambada contest. Even untrained, dancing was in Perez's blood. The recognition at the national contest earned young Perez enough acknowledgment for him to be admitted into one of Cali's most exceptional dance academies. As a return courtesy, he taught step aerobics at the school.

In 1999, Perez relocated to Miami, Florida, where he aspired to earn a living by teaching and performing dance and aerobics. This combination, coupled with a 2003 infomercial, resulted in his rise to popularity. There is a good chance that you have seen a video, taken a class, or exercised to his teaching. Alberto Perez is the creator of the widespread sensation called Zumba.

According to an October 2014 article in Bloomsburg Businessweek, there has been a notable rise in the number of job hunters who are listing unique "soft" skills on their profiles and resumes to attract potential employers. LinkedIn.com, a career website with over 313 million users, reports that many people are pitching abilities on their profiles. Sixty percent of all LinkedIn users are posting CPR as one of those skills. With the enhanced power to dig deeper into the lives of potential employees using technology, there is a growing population of job seekers who are including hobbies and interests on their electronic resumes. Korean culture is listed by 26% of users, men's fashion by 25%, and, amazingly, Zumba, a craze that has been in existence since only 2003, is highlighted by 24%. According to LinkedIn, when a person places interests and hobbies on their resume, they receive thirteen more online hits per day.

How does the skill of understanding Zumba help you get a job? The industrialized world is widely data driven. Prospective employers do not need to shuffle through a lot of paper and weed through hundreds of resumes to find qualified applicants. Individuals who are hiring simply need to fill out a profile, then quickly narrow down potential candidates using database queries. More frequently, employers are studying the skill sets of prospective employees. Knowing something about a candidate's personal life gives the employer the opportunity to understand whether the candidate will fit into the chemistry and culture of their company. Fourteen million people take Zumba classes in 185 countries at 140,000 different locations. That is an extensive network of Zumba followers. The odds are high that if a person exercises to Zumba, it will not take them long to find another person interested in Zumba as well.

Paul McCartney exercises to Zumba. However, his association with music is most likely what most people talk with him about. Hypothetically, what if Zumba was one of your interests, and you knew McCartney shared this interest? A conversational bond about Zumba would make a deeper connection and a memorable conversation. What if the person standing in line at that teashop was not Paul McCartney, but rather a prospective employer? If that employer could tap into your personal life to discover that Zumba is a commonality you both share, will this affect potential employment? Do you think your stock just rose? What gets people hired for a job? Every employer wants an employee with competence in the role to which they are hiring. Job skills are "hard skills." Hard skills are normally gained through classical training in a school or apprenticeship; incidentally, these are also the skills that standardized tests seek to evaluate. However, soft skills, including interests and hobbies, often leave potential employers saying, "I really could connect with him." What do you think this connection is generated by—soft or hard skills?

(2)

*"He who says he can, and he who says he can't, is probably right."*

—*Confucius*

IN 1917, EIGHT-YEAR-OLD Glenn Cunningham, his parents, and his thirteen-year-old brother were living in Elkhart, Kansas. He attended a one room schoolhouse. Most schoolhouses were heated by coal and wood. If the school was going to be warm in the winter, someone would have to get a fire started before the day could begin. Glenn's wintertime duty was to go to school early on cold mornings, and fill and light the potbelly stove with his brother's help. Often, the wood was hard to ignite, so kerosene was used as an accelerant. One early fall day, Glenn went to light the fire with his brother, and everything in his life changed. An explosion ripped through the schoolhouse. Someone had inadvertently replaced the kerosene with gasoline. As help arrived, a nearly dead Glenn was dragged from the burning structure. His brother perished.

Glenn was rushed to a local hospital. The extent of Glenn's injuries was so severe that most doctors who saw Glenn informed his mother that he would most certainly die. Burns from the fire completely removed all the flesh from both of his knees and his shins. He lost all the toes on his left foot. The transverse arch of that left foot was destroyed. More than one doctor said it would be best if Glenn would die. He was in unbelievable pain, and all the people that examined him were convinced that he would be permanently disabled and never walk again. The doctors at the hospital recommended that his legs should be amputated, but Glenn's exasperated distress caused his parents to refuse this surgery. If the doctors had known what was to come, amputation would have never been a consideration.

Glenn Cunningham would have to endure two years of physical therapy before he was able to attempt to take his first steps. Glenn's family were devout Christians, and he grew fond of Bible verse Isaiah 40:31: "But those who wait on the Lord shall renew their strength; they shall mount up like eagles, they shall run and not be weary, they shall walk and not faint." Miraculously, two years after the fire, Glenn began to walk again.

The 1936 Olympics were held in Berlin, Germany. This would be the Olympics in which Jesse Owens became a running legend, defying the Aryan vision of Adolf Hitler. Owens would win four gold medals in the 100-meter dash, the 200-meter dash, the 4x100-meter relay, and the long jump. Owen's teammate was toeless and scarred Glenn Cunningham. Just two years prior, Cunningham would set the world record for the mile with 4 minutes, 6.8 seconds. This record would stand for nearly three years. In track and field, the milestone of eclipsing the 4-minute mark in the mile was a goal that was not thought of as attainable. However, many believed that if this milestone were to be reached, Cunningham would be the first to run a 4-minute mile, but he maintained a fear of falling by running full speed for an entire mile. Cunningham would habitually stay with a leader in a race, then sprint the final 100 meters, so his full potential may have never been tested. In 1936, Glenn Cunningham, a man with no toes on his left foot and extensive scarring from the burns he sustained when he was eight, would cross the finish line in the 1,500 meters in second place, winning a silver medal. Later that year, Cunningham would set the world record at the 800-meter distance. Following the 1936 Olympics, Cunningham's team of Olympians would vote him Most Popular Athlete.

Cunningham's story seems miraculous, but his against all odds narrative has a practical message as well. Cunningham allowed his most significant obstacle in life to be his greatest asset. If he had merely become the world's greatest miler and a silver medalist, his story would evaporate into the shadows of the hundreds of people who have achieved Olympic success. Instead, his achievements have only been made more impressive by the special adversity he faced along the way. Life is easy and satisfying when winning is part of it. It is easy to stay positive in the face of success. However, the actual colors of a person's character are challenged in the face of adversity. Resiliency will not always lead to the Olympics, but it does promote success.

This chapter opened with an interview with Nicole Dreiske. In Dreiske's interview, she acknowledged that she grew through the experience of having a teacher that was not afraid to give her talented students grades below what they were used to getting. That teacher posed challenges. In Dreiske's case, much like Cunningham's, challenges did not have to define a person. If facing a challenge is regularly practiced, working through challenges becomes easier. Ultimately, working through opposition makes people more prepared to succeed.

If you were an employer, would you want to hire Glenn Cunningham? Would his ability to overcome obstacles increase success in the workplace? Absolutely! Why? Because, in the face of significant obstacles, Cunningham was successful. Every job has some challenges. Would the soft skill of resiliency be just as important as the "hard skill," which is specific to the task?

In a 1990s interview, actor Will Smith stated that there is no such thing as a plan B. Smith's point is plan A is what you want, so why would you ever consider plan B? Having a plan B only allows obstacles to stand in your way. How do the greatest obstacles get overcome? They are conquered by not letting those challenges be roadblocks in the first place. More than likely, Glenn Cunningham saw his situation differently than we might. Cunningham proved that life's obstacles and challenges do not have to define you.

(3)

THERE ARE INSTANCES where snap decisions have significant consequences; a quick turn out into traffic, catching oneself when tripping on stairs, and so on. Sometimes, change is so rapid that there is no time to prepare. Adaptation is essential to survive gradual change, but it also is equally valuable when it comes to snap decision making.

On October 13th, 1972, the Old Christian Club Rugby Union Team from Uruguay was flying above the Andes Mountains en route to play in a match in Santiago, Chile. The Andes Mountains create unpredictable weather and thick cloud cover. The flight was already delayed by a day, and with the pressing importance of the upcoming rugby scrum, pilots decided to fly through a lesser traveled mountain pass to get to Chile. The Andes Mountains are tall, with the highest peak, Aconcagua, reaching a remarkable 22,841 feet above sea level. The elevation of this section of the mountains is so high that it affects the weather across South America. The weather on the Argentine-Chilean border creates ecological diversity where rain forests exist within miles of glaciers; these glaciers can cause trouble by creating blizzard conditions that reverse to pouring rain within an hour.

There, above this treacherous terrain, flew the Uruguayan rugby team, some family members, and a crew of five. Operating high above the clouds allowed for visibility, but eventually, the plane had to descend into the clouds and fly blind. In 1972, plane speed was charted with terrain maps, so if a pilot was flying blind, they still could descend safely based on mathematical calculations combined with maps.

As the Uruguayan Air Force jet descended blindly, the crew failed to consider the strong headwinds. When they were cleared to descend, they were unknowingly flying over 13,000-foot mountain peaks. The plane dropped and flew right into the side of a mountain. Flight 571 crashed at 11,800 feet on a mountain so remote that it was unnamed. Initially, 29 of the passengers survived, but the crash was in an untraveled, poorly mapped, and virtually unexplored mountainous area. The last radioed location was miscalculated by over one hundred miles. Sixteen days later, an avalanche would take eight more lives. In the end, sixteen of the original forty-five passengers would survive a seventy-two-day ordeal before being rescued. Nobody on the flight had trained for this type of situation; they lacked hard survival or mountaineering skills. How those final survivors endured would require every soft skill each member possessed.

The final rescue of the sixteen living passengers was the result of decisions made by two of the surviving rugby players. Roberto Canessa and Nando Parrado ascended a 15,000-foot mountain in search of help. Miscalculations led the survivors to believe that they were nearly out of the Andes, but when the two reached the 15,000-foot peak, all they saw was an endless horizon of mountains. Eventually, Canessa and Parrado found a valley, which led them to civilization.

In 2006, Nando Parrado published a book about the horrific experience. The motivation behind his book was unconventional. It was written out of the frustration surrounding his internal turmoil of survival being viewed by the general public as an adventure of national pride. Parrado wanted to emphasize that there was no glory in this tragedy, and his story was one of horror and ugliness.

What kept the sixteen people alive on that mountain peak for seventy-two days was a combination of luck and the soft skills of the survivors. The initial death toll from the accident was twelve, and the avalanche took eight more. That left twenty-five adults, sixteen of which would survive the ordeal for seventy-two days with injuries including broken legs. Ingenuity played an instrumental role. Bones were splinted with the wreckage from the plane. To avoid snow blindness, Adolfo Stauch created mountaineering goggles fashioned from the sun visors in the cockpit. Exposure to the extreme cold needed to be dealt with immediately. The survivors realized that it was safer to wait by the wreckage than to attempt hiking to the west through the Andes Mountains. Daytime temperatures were above freezing, but nighttime temperatures dropped low enough to take a person's life. To keep the cold at bay, the survivors turned to the wreckage of the plane; they found layers of quilted batts of insulation in the tail section to create sleeping bags, and the wreckage itself could help somewhat with the wind. For Canessa and Parrado, the sleeping bags were the key to their survival.

With their warmth assured, the survivors turned to the danger of starvation. They tried eating strips of leather from luggage and tore out seat cushions hoping to find edible straw padding. There was no food. After every other option was exhausted, they had to resort to cannibalism. Though the survivors understood that this was the only remaining option, it must have been unimaginably difficult; many of the survivors knew the dead. Some of them were family members and friends. However, the decision to resort to cannibalism saved the lives of the sixteen. After the rescue, none of the families of the deceased challenged these decisions.

If you were a business owner, would you hire one of the survivors of this plane crash? Would this story matter in your decision?

Sixteen survivors possessed the ability to make the most difficult of decisions. They faced the moral implications of cannibalism, yet they were able to make a group decision, and that decision allowed them to survive seventy-two days in the high reaches of the Andes Mountains. They possessed perseverance and the resolution to live. The survivors maximized their resourcefulness, fashioning sleeping bags, goggles, and a shelter from the little that they had. It sustained them for over ten weeks. Spurred on by these tools, two of the survivors were able to make the journey to save them all.

How do we know when we are around a successful person? Initially, we do not. Only time and shared experiences reveal soft skills. When we are electing our leaders, hiring employees, or trusting teachers, how do we know if the person we are looking at will head in a fruitful direction? At first, I would guess that the survivors of Flight 571 asked the same question. Though it takes years to know a person, an advertisement of soft skills may help expedite the process.

(4)

THE ITALIAN SCULPTOR and artist Michelangelo once stated, "A man paints with his brains and not with his hands." Michelangelo understood and believed that the possibilities for the mind to expand are far greater than the physical abilities of the human body. What would Michelangelo have said if he knew that humans have two brains? The first brain is what we traditionally think of: the one in our head. Our thoughts, memories, and actions are almost exclusively controlled by this near infinite cluster of neurons.

The gut of a person has its own, second "mind" that is referred to as the enteric nervous system, or ENS. Like the brain in a person's head, the ENS dispatches and receives messages through nerve impulses, records experiences, and responds to emotions. The ENS is in the sheaths lining the digestive system, and it can operate independently from the brain. It can only be hypothesized what role the "gut brain" could have played in ancestors of human beings. The ENS contains nerves identified as glial cells, which nourish neurons and activate cells that are involved in immune responses. The nerves have sensors that detect sugar, proteins, and many other nutrients that require monitoring during digestion. They have a secondary function as well. When the brain in our head senses different stimuli, it releases hormones. Imagine the sensation in the belly when taking a challenging test. Seconds before the exam is administered, there is an anxious sensation described as "butterflies" in the stomach. The butterfly feeling is caused by hormones directly affecting the enteric nervous system.

The vagus nerve connects the ENS to our brain. Impulses travel through this nerve between the heart, mind, and the digestive system. Along with butterflies, the overstimulation of this nerve increases heart rate. Increased nerve activity also affects the urinary system, which explains why people fear they may lose control of their bladder.

Most modern offices rely heavily on technology through electronic networks. Unexpected network outages cause panic. In this fast-paced world, when lightning-fast speeds of systems come to a grinding halt, anxiety goes up. The natural solution to solve network issues is to have a team of techies that have the hard skills to fix the problems. What if the hard skills that the techies possess are not enough to solve the problem? What is the result? Anxiety, frustration, and panic potentially start to travel throughout the company. As each person in the company reacts, hormone messengers are sent from the brain through the vagus nerve and go rapidly toward the enteric nervous system. Some people have greater control of this and are in tune with their "gut brain," but many people are not. Our rational mind often contradicts the 'thoughts' within our gut. So being calm under pressure also involves the soft skill of being able to control reactions through the vagus nerve.

Bacteria in the gut can have a direct effect on the ENS. When food does not digest well, it causes widespread sickness throughout the body. There are more neurons in the sheath surrounding the digestive tract than the whole peripheral nervous system. The neuroscience behind gastrointestinal distress or simply an upset stomach says that once one part of the enteric nervous system is sensing problems, it communicates impulses through the vagus nerve to the brain. The brain is rational, and once it detects the signals from the enteric nervous system, a series of reactions take place.

Emeran Mayer is a professor at the University of California's Geffen School of Medicine. He studies the nerve fibers in the gut. According to Mayer, 90% of the traffic on the vagus nerve is impulses sent from the gut to the brain. It seems more logical that the mind should be controlling the gut, but Mayer's research suggests that this may not be the case. The impulses of the "gut brain" can control the mind. Mayer asserts that the result of this interaction can cause turmoil: moods can sour, and a person's emotional well-being can be compromised when our gut brain is not in harmony with our mind. Many remedies for depression include chemical and electrical stimulation of the vagus nerve. So incidentally, many treatments for depression cause changes or sensations in the gastrointestinal tract through the vagus nerve.

There is a connection between the ENS, Glenn Cunningham's story, and the soft skill of knowing Zumba. In the case of Cunningham, he had natural resilience. He refused to let a catastrophic obstacle stand in his way. People who exercise to such activities as Zumba are often passionate about it. Passion, resilience, and tenacity are all developed by the control of gut impulses. Employers want employees with resilience, shared interests, and excellent instincts—all soft skills. An employee like that is invaluable. Soft skills directly relate to the bits of intelligence needed to perform a job well. Often these skills are overlooked, especially when hiring, because hard skills match the job the person is interviewing for. However, soft skills have the wide-scale potential to create success. They promote a positive and productive workplace.

Should soft skills be ignored? What does your gut say? Is the best way to predict the success of potential employees made through a resume and some letters of recommendation? Does the tailoring of the questions in an interview matter? Often job applications are laden with requirements for concrete evidence of hard skills, but soft skills paint an accurate picture of potential success, too. So, should you list Zumba—or any soft skills—on your resume? Tradition says no, but the chance for a successful match between a place of employment and a candidate increases when a candidate shares a standard connection. Have a vision, and do not be afraid to change.

(5)

SPORTS JUNKIES LOVE to compare athletes and their statistics. Is it possible to identify the greatest all-time athletes in all sports? Considering some athletes played in different eras, on various surfaces against other athletes, comparisons are nearly impossible. A baseball player from the 1920s cannot be resurrected from the dirt to pitch in a game with players of today. However, beyond statistics, there is something that can be compared: skills.

Current baseball players are world class athletes with individual skill sets that may put old timers to shame. Does that mean that if you put Derek Jeter at his prime in a 1927 Yankees uniform and Babe Ruth into today's game, one would have a better success based on athletic ability? Most ballplayers nowadays are bigger, faster, and stronger. Babe Ruth, at his prime, was roughly 215 pounds and 6 foot 2 inches tall. He was one of the most prominent ballplayers of his day. Derek Jeter, the retired Yankee shortstop, is 6 foot 5 inches. This is not unusual. Are modern ballplayers better than the players of years ago, or does it all boil down to simple facts and skill?

Skills exist either because of natural ability or are learned by extensive practice. At its most basic definition, a skill is something that a person is required to do to complete a task. Modern ballplayers are highly specialized. The designated hitter does not have to play the field. His job is uncomplicated; he simply hits the ball. The designated hitter was added to baseball in 1973. Most players of yesteryear had to pitch and hit; this is nearly unheard of today. Even in the National League, where pitchers are required to hit, a pitcher hitting a meager .200 is desirable. Pitchers in the National League are often asked to bunt to advance a baserunner. Their importance on the field is to throw the baseball hard and deceive the batter.

However, these expectations were not always the norm. Babe Ruth's focus early in his career was pitching. From 1915 to 1918 he posted a major league pitching record of 78-40, and of the 142 games he started, he completed 107 by pitching all nine innings. Today, it is a rarity for a pitcher to complete a game twice within a season. The yesteryear game of baseball required Babe Ruth to have multiple hard skills. When the Yankees acquired Babe Ruth from the Boston Red Sox, they already had an established group of pitchers. Since he had many different hard skills, he was able to continue to develop as a successful hitter. As a Yankee, he only pitched 31 innings, winning five games over a 15-year tenure. In 1920, his first year with the Yankees, he hit fifty-four home runs, which is a tidy sum even by today's standards.

The Cy Young Award is presented to a pitcher voted on by the Baseball Writers' Association of America, a group with one representative from each team. This award identifies the best pitcher by consensus vote in major league baseball each year. Cy Young's career spanned from 1890 to 1911. In 1903, he batted .321 with a

.431 slugging percentage. Conversely, the 2014 National League batting champ was Justin Morneau, who hit a .319 batting average. Moreover, in the same season, Clayton Kershaw of the Los Angeles Dodgers posted twenty-one wins, the most in the majors. Cy Young, in comparison, won twenty-eight games in that 1903 season. Twenty-three of the twenty-five pitchers to ever throw over 375 innings in a season played from 1901 to 1917. The 2014 leader of the most innings pitched was David Price with 248-1/3 innings.

A natural conclusion is that ballplayers of today who specialize in one hard skill should have inflated statistics compared to ballplayers of long ago who depended on many hard skills. They do not. In the earliest days of baseball, things were not as controlled as they are for players today. For example, in 2013, Stephen Strasburg, arguably the most talented strikeout pitcher that year, was shut down after an inning limit was reached based on calculated risk. His team, the Washington Nationals, was still in contention to make the playoffs. One may assume that this practice would not have occurred in the early 1900s due to less data on rehabilitation from injuries. Dizzy Dean, who pitched for the Chicago Cubs, won twenty-four games in one season; in that same season, he had eleven saves. This means he finished games that other people started. Today, it is unheard of for a starter to also close games. Of course, owners and managers have a more significant financial stake than they did years ago; until the late 1970s, when Reggie Jackson signed the first million-dollar contract, most major league baseball players earned so little that they worked odd jobs in the offseason. Babe Ruth's highest salary was $80,000, whereas today's major league minimum salary is over half a million dollars.

Ty Cobb, who hit a lifetime batting average of .366 (the highest of all time), also threw some innings on the mound. He also stole bases, and he is the all-time leader of stealing home plate with 54 bases. In 1915 alone, he stole a total of ninety-six bases.

It may seem reasonable that most of the old timers may be way overwhelmed in today's Major Leagues. Today's pitchers would overpower hitters of the past based on sheer size. Though it cannot be fully confirmed due to the lack of technology, only three pitchers, Walter Johnson, Bob Feller, and Steve Dalkowski, threw over 100 miles per hour before 1960. By contrast, in 2019 alone, over seven players active in the Major Leagues threw over 100 miles per hour. Still, it would be unfair to sell the old timers short. What use would a pitcher who only throws one inning every two days be in the early 1900s? Many of the hardest throwing pitchers are closers. They may only throw 20 pitches in a game. Johnson, Feller, and Dalkowski were all expected to start and finish games. Today's ballplayers specialize in skills to face specific hitters and pitchers.

Skill sets change as jobs evolve. In any career, including major league baseball, the skill set required in today's world may be significantly different from decades ago. Major league baseball teaches us that different eras call on different skill sets. This is consistent with most professions. The one room schoolhouse changed with the development of transportation and the growth of populations to eventually become what we see today. At one time, a teacher may have been responsible for educating children of all ages in the same classroom; now, teachers usually teach at a single grade level and specialize in individual subjects. Successful people recognize these changing skill sets, and they either evolve or fade into oblivion. In the animal world, we would call this adaptability, or survival of the fittest.

Careers can span half of a lifetime. Though people must readjust to change, as long as a person remains alert and willing, appropriate actions can be taken. Changes may happen quickly or slowly. The 1973 introduction of the designated hitter in the American League of major league baseball caused managers to adapt promptly by creating new strategies to win ballgames. Successful people know how to adapt.

(6)

PRESIDENT THEODORE ROOSEVELT had severe juvenile asthma. Some doctors questioned whether he would live to adulthood. Roosevelt is the consummate underdog; he was the weak boy who went on to become the leader of the Rough Riders and the President of the United States. Roosevelt's experience as a child had a profound effect on his interest when pushing the limits in both the wilderness and the White House. As a child, Roosevelt was a target for bullies, and to help him develop the strength to fight back, his father purchased him boxing lessons. As a teen, Roosevelt was told that due to heart problems, he should be limited to a desk job to avoid the strenuous life, but Roosevelt refused to succumb to working from a chair. Roosevelt worked out, exercised regularly, and boxed into his adulthood. People boxed with the President of the United States! In fact, as president, he continued sparring with partners until he took a blow that would detach his left retina. This incident left President Teddy Roosevelt blind in one eye.

When the odds are stacked against some people, they get stronger. The notion defies logic. Roosevelt's active life was driven by the soft skills of survival, work ethic, and leadership. His most potent speech, written in 1905, was entitled "The Strenuous Life." If you were challenged to live a strenuous life, your task would be to live a life of hard work, contribution, and action. Would you want to be around a person leading a strenuous life? Does an active life lead to a life of fulfillment? According to Roosevelt, it does.

Teddy Roosevelt, the boy who was deemed too unhealthy for physical work, successfully led the Rough Riders in the Spanish American War and took over the country after President McKinley was assassinated. In 1905, the labor riots and strikes that were tearing Chicago apart certainly concerned him, but they did not intimidate him. The events of Chicago set the stage for Roosevelt to speak out about the character of successful people. That year, he delivered his speech titled "The Strenuous Life." Early on in Roosevelt's speech, he pinpointed work ethic, a soft skill, and its value: "I wish to preach, not the doctrine of the ignoble ease, but the doctrine of the strenuous life, the life of toil and effort, of labor and strife; to preach the highest form of success which comes, not to the man who desires mere easy peace, but to the man who does not shrink from danger, from hardship, or from bitter toil, and who out of these wins the splendid ultimate triumph."

Roosevelt valued soft skills. He stayed close to the ideals of living the life of a person committed to hard work and called out people who sat back and lived a life of ease. He appreciated people who were committed to effort when faced with a challenge. Because of his values, Roosevelt would have embraced the story of the Andes survivors, and he reminds us that the reward for living a life of fulfillment and hard work is the ultimate triumph. The catalyst for Roosevelt's speech was the labor issue in Chicago. It targeted people whom he saw as lazy and not doing their part to contribute to an evolving society.

Is living the doctrine of a strenuous life timeless? Work ethic and the ability to face challenges are both soft skills, and they are often on the road less traveled. History tells us that those who have the skills to stay the course, even in the face of large-scale adversity, often go on to achieve great things. Dr. Seuss's first children's book, "And to Think I Saw It on Mulberry Street," sold over 6 million copies after 27 publishers rejected it. Heisman Trophy winner Hershel Walker was told by his high school coach to run track because he was too small to play football. Years of intense training put him on top of the college football world. Douglas MacArthur was turned down for admission into West Point, but on his third try, he succeeded. Rodin, the sculptor of *The Thinker*, was called an idiot by his father and uneducable by his uncle. Men and women who overcome adversity and work through an active life to achieve their goals provide us with the models for advancement. Time after time, people living against tremendous odds overcome challenges by not listening to those who pointed out the obstacles. They found success by living a strenuous life.

(7)

ALWAYS BE OPEN to the truth, even if it contradicts years of institutionalization. Democracy did not start on the North American continent with the colonial rebellion against the British. Democracy was born in upstate New York with the unification of a small group of small Native American nations. Dekanawida was regularly referred to as the Great Peacemaker by the Haudenosaunee (Iroquois) Nation of upstate New York. Most Native American history is recorded through oral tradition; therefore, the exact history of his life can differ from one source to the next. Most agree that he was living in upstate New York in 1451 based on the fact that his appearance was consistent in many accounts with the identification of a solar eclipse. Dekanawida was a Native American born on the shores of Lake Ontario and was most likely a Huron. However, some oral accounts place him initially with the Oneida Nation, one of the six nations bound together as the Iroquois. His ability to unify people could be likened to Lincoln's ability to unify a fractured country during the Civil War. He preached peace and saw the importance of unification. Because of this, he is referred to as the Great Peacemaker more often than by his actual name.

Dekanawida took an interest in a cluster of fragmented tribes in upstate New York. They would become the Haudenosaunee or, as the French called them, the Iroquois. He saw the potential for a great nation if the smaller nations would unify through peace. The Seneca, Cayuga, Onondaga, Oneida, and Mohawk were vulnerable, warring against each other in their split state. Dekanawida had a solid vision of peace, but due to a grossly disfigured face, which caused a speech impediment, he was not fully received or understood.

Hiawatha was a politically savvy orator and was a disciple of Dekanawida. His soft skill of communication complimented Dekanawida, who had a gifted and peaceful mind. They worked together to teach the Iroquois that peace made them stronger. They gathered leaders at the home of Jigonhsasee, who lived along one of the commonly traveled war paths near the shores of Onondaga Lake. She made the conscious decision to offer anyone hospitality, no matter what tribe they came from. Her home was the ideal location for the Iroquois leaders to assemble because it was a place of no judgment.

Influenced by the ideas of Dekanawida, Hiawatha spent time working with all leaders of the Haudenosaunee. In front of the chiefs of all five nations, he took one arrow and demonstrated its weakness by snapping it in half. Then he bundled five arrows, each symbolizing different nations, and demonstrated the strength of unification with his inability to snap the shafts. If you look at the American bald eagle's talon, it holds thirteen arrows demonstrating the strength of the unification of the original thirteen states. This American symbol was adapted from the Iroquois.

Dekanawida and Hiawatha's campaign grew. They were able to convince most chiefs to become stronger through peace, but one leader refused to listen to their message. Tadodaho was the most brutal and feared leader and tyrannically ruled the Onondaga Nation. The Native Americans used oral tradition to pass along their history, so today he is depicted as a Medusa-like character.

Modern folklorists describe Tadodaho as having snakes growing from his head and a withered body with many twists. Why he would not move towards peace is unknown, but Tadodaho was responsible for the death of one or more of Hiawatha's daughters. Despite his anger, Hiawatha remained committed to peace for the greater good. After much effort, Tadodaho was swayed to become peaceful. To commemorate the unity, Dekanawida and Hiawatha brought the fifty chiefs from the Haudenosaunee together on the shores of Lake Oneida. Each chief placed a hatchet in a large hole and buried it beneath a white pine tree. This is where the term bury the hatchet originates. It is used today to suggest an end to conflict, whether that conflict is a simple argument or a full-blown war. Each nation appointed ten chiefs to represent their nations, and the first democracy on the North American continent was born.

The Founding Fathers of the United States were very aware of the political structure of many of the Native American tribes, and the Iroquois assembly influenced early American leaders in the writing of the Constitution. In July of 1754 at the Albany Congress, Benjamin Franklin said of the Iroquois Confederacy: "It would be a strange thing… if six nations [the Tuscarora tribe joined the Iroquois in 1722] of ignorant savages should be capable of forming such a union, and yet it has subsisted for ages and appears in-dissolvable, and yet like a union should be impractical for ten or a dozen English colonies." Franklin's quote is evidence that even though he did not directly see a correlation between the political structure of the Iroquois and its application on the central government of the colonies, he was considering the working establishment of Native American democracies.

Once peace had been achieved, Hiawatha commemorated the event with a ceremonial wampum belt of purple and white clam shells, showing the unity between the tribes. Then, to ensure that the peace would last, Dekanawida set in motion a series of laws by which the Iroquois would live. Six hundred and fifty years later, the Iroquois are still living by the laws from the 15th century. Clan mothers choose their male counterparts to lead as chiefs. When decisions are made as a council, there is no voting based on majority; all decisions are to be arrived at by unanimous decision. All ideas and principles are discussed, and opinions are considered. There is a considerable difference between democracy and total autonomy. There are no political parties in the Iroquois. It is rare that a single person can make effective decisions, empower change, and win over the minds of others. In the case of the Iroquois, the peaceful and moral mind of Dekanawida needed to be coupled with the soft skills of the great communicator, Hiawatha. Their example has led to the long-lasting political structure of a completely autonomous democracy. Communication, empathy, tolerance, and patience are all soft skills that are necessary for this system to be successful.

Most western schools spend an enormous amount of time and money testing hard skills with little attention to soft skills. They test reading, writing, and mathematics. While it is true that these are essential hard skills, students are not evaluated on interpersonal skills, work ethic, tenacity, or intuition. When people are hired, companies look at resumes of hard skills to narrow candidates down. But what if this system is eliminating the best team players, motivators, and those with strong work ethic by only looking at hard skills?

Louis Pasteur is the poster child for this scenario. Pasteur was an undergraduate in Dijon, France and scored 15th in a class of 22. At this academic rank, there are very few medical schools in the world that would take him seriously, but his understanding of fermentation and diseases was extraordinary; it is from him that we get the process of pasteurization. His soft skill of creativity could have been overlooked due to his lack of pure academia. How many illnesses and deaths have been prevented by the practice of pasteurization? Pasteur's procedure of pasteurization has also increased the shelf life of dairy products.

In the business world, leadership and stockholders are fixated on the bottom line. Profits are important, meaning that many companies live only in the here and now. They bank on the hard skills offered by the current cutting-edge employees, but if businesses expect to survive, they have to invest in a complex combination of diverse employees with soft and hard skills. Business is like a Halloween bucket full of chocolate. Almost every person enjoys that first piece of chocolate. Often a second and third are enjoyed too. If chocolate symbolizes hard skills, what happens when it is eaten? By the fourth, fifth and sixth pieces, the chocolate becomes rough, and by piece number twenty, the chocolate has a reverse effect. It becomes sickening. Such is the case with skills. Whether hard or soft, too much of one skill creates a burden. Whether in a school, government, business, or family, a well-rounded, diverse, and balanced structure is necessary to increase the probability of success.

# Interview with Homer Hickam
July 23, 2018
Huntsville, Alabama

*I met Homer Hickam at the United States Rocketry Center after he did a presentation about the real story behind his book, Rocket Boys. This book was made into the movie October Sky. Hickam is an American author, Vietnam veteran, and a former NASA engineer. He trained astronaut crews for numerous Spacelab and Space Shuttle missions, including the development of the Hubble Space Telescope. Hickam's final work for NASA was as the Payload Training Manager for the International Space Station program.*

**Albrecht:** I'm standing with…

**Hickam:** Homer Hickam.

**Albrecht:** Can you tell me a little bit about yourself, Homer.

**Hickam:** Well, um, I am primarily known for a book called *Rocket Boys*, which was turned into the movie, *October Sky*. I used to be a NASA engineer. These days I write for a living, but I've done a number of things during my life.

**Albrecht**: That's excellent. How old are you?

**Hickam:** I'm seventy-five years old.

**Albrecht:** You don't look seventy-five years old.

**Hickam:** Well, I appreciate that.

**Albrecht:** Would you please describe your favorite teacher?

**Hickam:** Right, my favorite teacher was Ms. Freida Riley, who was our science, physics, and chemistry teacher in high school. That was Big Creek High School in back in West Virginia in the late-1950s, and Ms. Riley encouraged a few young boys to do a lot more than they thought they could possibly do, and that is from Southern West Virginia to go off to the National Science Fair and win the darn thing by building advanced, very advanced rockets.

**Albrecht:** Were you one of those boys?

**Hickam:** I was one of those boys, and Ms. Riley was… she was very willing to fight for her boys. She fought for us to get advanced math classes. She went up against a very tough school and the administration, a very strong principal, and all the way up to the county board of education. She fought for her boys. She fought for all of her students. Ultimately, she succumbed to Hodgkin's disease, which was fatal back during those days, but to the very end, she was a teacher. She insisted on being carried to her classes… on a stretcher at the very end, and she taught right up to the day she died.

**Albrecht:** That's amazing. Three words that would describe her…

**Hickam:** Wonderful. Inspirational. Loving.

### Reflection:

Great teachers fearlessly advocate for their students. Homer Hickam's memories of his favorite educator teach us about the power of advocacy. Ms. Freida Riley left this Earth 58 years before

Hickam's account, but she is alive in Hickam's heart and mind. Ms. Riley embraced her students to the point that she wanted to be their teacher to the very end. She did not just want to be a teacher; she needed to be at school.

Homer Hickam's story about Ms. Riley shows us that profoundly influential teachers live their responsibility. Teaching is much more than a job. It is a lifestyle. Of course, everybody's life is different. There have been circumstances in my life when I could not come in early or stay late because my children were young. Teachers do have lives. However, exceptional educators devote countless extra hours outside of the regular school day on behalf of their students when their lives allow them to. Teachers go to baseball games, dance recitals, soccer contests, and occasionally show up for a pet's funeral. Excellent educators do not live nine to five. They are teachers twenty-four hours a day, seven days a week.

I maintain the philosophy that there is no such thing as a bad year of school. Admittedly, there are years that I am more tired than others, but a child does not have a second chance at a school year. Therefore, each year has to be unique and treated like it is special because, indeed, it is. A classroom, for better or for worse, is similar to a family. The rocket boys all went to school together. This group of young men from Big Creek, West Virginia was a tight-knit family. They stayed bonded by a common interest in science, but without any resources, this group of West Virginians most likely would have never worked for NASA and may have never felt the level of success that they did through learning and experimenting with rocketry. Ms. Riley demanded that the young men she was preparing for the world be entitled to not only her support, but the support of the community, school, and administration. Ms. Riley was a rule breaker. She knew that traditional education was not going to work for her class. She recognized the talent, interest, and potential in all of her students and became their advocate. In the 2010 census, Big Creek, West Virginia had a population of 237. It is a tiny town. Resources and experiences are limited in towns of this size. Ms. Riley had the mindset that part of her job was to expose the world's opportunities to her students. Where a person is born does not have to limit their dreams or define them.

Excellent advocates make great teachers. Ms. Riley had her naysayers, but they did not sway her. In her eyes, the advancement of each of her students had to take top priority. She believed in plan A, and most likely did not have a plan B. Hickam chose to describe Ms. Riley as inspirational. Advocacy creates opportunities, and those students who are supported, get inspired.

I spent the week before December 17th, 2003 in the Outer Banks of North Carolina where, one-hundred years prior, the Wright Brothers flew the first airplane. In December of 2003, the Wright Brothers National Memorial site was bustling. Famous aviators from all over the globe were there to share ideas, present, and take in the celebration of the anniversary of one of man's greatest achievements: mechanical powered flight. Neil Armstrong and Buzz Aldrin both delivered speeches. President George W. Bush flew in on Marine I, and a group of scientists made a replica of the 1903 Wright Flyer and attempted to operate it. Mother Nature did not cooperate. Just like the Wright Brothers, these scientists needed wind to fly. December 17th, 2003 was a dreary, cold, and rainy day. It was not flying weather. Nevertheless, the designers of the replica gave flight a try. The plane may have been off the ground for a second before it pitched to the right, digging into the mud. It did not matter; the crowd roared, and for a few minutes, everyone got to hear the unique noise that wooden biplane propellers make.

NASA was represented at the Wright Brothers' 100th anniversary of flight. By 2003, the Space Shuttle had flown 113 of its 120 missions. The United States had successfully landed six manned missions on the moon. Before December 17th, 1903, a human flight could only be imagined. The Wright Brothers opened up a new frontier: the skies.

Dan Berry is an astronaut that flew on three Space Shuttle missions and has accumulated over twenty-four hours of spacewalking experience. He presented multiple times during the 100th anniversary. Many of his presentations were about his perception and thoughts about the first missions to Mars. His mindset was a lot like that of Ms. Riley; he talked about recognizing the giftedness within students and the positive consequences of introducing young minds to vibrant ideas.

When Ms. Riley lived, nobody had ever traveled into space. But of course, that did not matter to her. What mattered was that her students got the opportunities and experiences necessary for them to fulfill their dreams. When I met Dan Berry, he made it known that he felt the same way. Berry's commentaries were inspiring, and each also presented new mindsets. Though he is an astronaut, physician, and engineer, he reminded me of a teacher. After Berry's fourth presentation, I introduced myself. All I wanted to know was when—that is, when in the future will the first person walk on Mars? He said with a bold and confident smile, "That human being already has been born."

That statement hit me like a bulldozer. Somewhere, there is a teacher with a student in their classroom who will grow up to be the first person to set foot on Mars. Ms. Riley proved that this student does not have to come from privilege or a big-dot place on a map. That student may be in my class, and since so much giftedness is yet to be discovered, there is no way to predict who that person is. Each child is capable of greatness. They need the desire and a teacher to help them along. Every person was a child once, bubbling with potential waiting for someone to recognize their gift.

## Chapter 4
## Harry Coover, Jack McKissick & Vision Value

(1)

FEED MY SOUL and tell me a story. A well-told tale is enduring and memorable. Classic fables and fairytales were written for children to stress values; the moral of the tale grows like a seed into a plant. Initially, a child may not understand the message, but with repetition the message becomes clear, and over time it subtly guides the individual. Stories teach us about moral values, such as knowing right from wrong, exercising moderation, and practicing honesty. The narratives that are passed down from generation to generation to provide consistency of cultural values.

The following story has many versions. The details and settings do not outweigh the moral message that is passed on. It is a classic illustration of transferred moral values through a story.

*A young Jewish gentleman went to his rabbi two weeks after he carried his newborn child home. The newborn had colic, and the young man was frazzled. Between the dog, his newborn son, and his wife, he felt he had no space in his house. The rabbi calmly stroked his long silvery beard and told the young man that his predicaments would be solved if he bought another dog. So, in faith, the young man went to a dog shelter and purchased an-*

*other dog. A week passed, and the young man revisited his rabbi. He said, "Rabbi, I bought a dog. Now one dog chases the other, and they bark so much the baby cries all of the time. My wife has bags under her eyes." The rabbi, again, smoothed his whiskers and instructed the man to purchase two cats. Obediently, the young man brought home two cats. A week later, he returned to the temple, more anxious than before, and stated, "Rabbi, I have bought a dog and two cats. The house smells, my wife is now irritated with me, and my child screams more than ever. I have no space." The rabbi went through the same routine of beard stroking with neutral expressions. He instructed the man to furnish his house with plants. Confused, the young man complied. Another week went by, and the young man was approaching desperation. "Rabbi," he stated, "you told me to buy plants. The cats climb the plants, and the dogs eat the leaves. The dogs get sick on the rug. My wife is ready to leave, and the baby never sleeps." "One last thing," stated the rabbi. "Buy a potbellied pig. Keep him in your family room." The man questioned his faith in the rabbi only for a second, then traveled to a farm and purchased the pig. The young man could not wait a week. Within days, he was back at the rabbi's residence. He restated to the rabbi that he had bought the dog, the plants, the cats, and the pig. His house smelled, his wife left to stay with her mother, and the kid was beyond help. Again, the rabbi stroked*

> his chin, but this time offered the man some alternative advice: "Sell the dogs, the cats, and the pig. Give away your plants and clean your house but keep your child and your wife." The man returned the following week happy because he only had to calm a crying baby.

The young man had a lot more space and far fewer difficulties than he had first thought. Narratives are teaching resources. Resources are all around us; human, natural, and manufactured. Often, we ignore the most fundamental of resources because they are not explicitly obvious. The young man in the story was blind to what he had. This tale reminds the reader that things can often be a lot more challenging than an individual believes. Resourcefulness has a direct effect on success, and a lack of resources challenges the progression toward success.

The Monday and Tuesday before Ash Wednesday make up a celebration in Trinidad and Tobago called Carnival. It was brought to the island nation by the French. Participants wear colorful costumes and parade in the streets; calypso and soca music in the air enhance limbo contests and dancing.

The history of drumming on Trinidad dates to before 1834, the year that slavery on the island was abolished. However, tensions still divided the races. The white population always disliked drumming. Slaves drummed a form of "Morse code" that communicated messages from slave to slave. Often, these messages were charged with put-downs directed at the slave owners. Drumming developed interaction between the black slave communities. When slavery was abolished, so many slaves had adopted drumming as a means of communication that it was included in the festivities during the Carnival celebration.

Colonists of the island became nervous that the drumming was being used to pass secret messages among the black populations, which escalated already high tensions between communities. Colonists feared that this type of unified communication would lead to revolution, and as a result, laws were passed that banned all drumming. The black population was not suppressed and turned to sticks called Tamboo Bamboo. Tamboo originated from the French name for drum or tambor. Sticks either struck the ground or were tapped together. In the 1930s, this transitioned into a form of "drumming" using biscuit tins that were hit with sticks. This became so popular that bands began adopting this technique—but music in Trinidad is rooted in gangs. Violence ensued, directly over music, which caused a ban of the Tamboo Bamboo. The intensity of the racial tensions became so heightened during Carnival that celebrations were banned during World War II. With the absence of bands, individual musical artists began experimenting privately.

Trinidad is home to many oil refineries. With 55-gallon oil drums in abundance, it was natural for oil drums to replace the biscuit cans. Elliot "Ellie" Mannette was one of the many individuals who experimented with sticks and oil drums. Mannette played in different bands in the Port of Spain—which is the capital of Trinidad and Tobago—before the ban on drumming. While experimenting, he discovered that distressing the lidded barrel on an oil drum produced a unique sound when tapped. This musician, who held a passion for metal tools, began exploring how tensions on the surface of drums would affect the sound. He fired his metal to improve the acoustic properties. Following World War II, Mannette took his steel band to Great Britain. The group was called TASPO (the Trinidad All Steel Percussion Orchestra). Mannette's work was such an immediate success that he was presented with offers to study at many different institutions, but he turned all of this down to build more steel pans. His innovations led him to be known as the father of the modern steel drum.

Traditional slave drumming used for communication, suppressed by people who were afraid of it, was revolutionized and transformed into what we know today as steel drum music. There are two aspects of this story that lay a foundation of consequence. First, the French felt frustration and fear of drumming music, so much so that they banned it. It is hard to conceptualize. As for the black slaves and former slave populations, they continued to improvise and adjust their approach to drumming as laws changed. The black community utilized the resources that were abundantly around them to enhance what they believed. They used biscuit cans, bamboo rods, and eventually 55-gallon oil drums to perfect and polish the art of drumming. They could have abandoned drumming altogether, or, as many other cultures had done, moved on to something else, conformed, or succumbed to oppression. The music on the radio today is not much different. A song gets popular, and everyone listens to it. Is this not conformity? However, the drumming of Trinidad was bound to the culture and experiences of an oppressed population of people, and they refused to conform. Instead, musicians became masters of the resources around them.

Resources surround us. They can be bought, traded for, and even found (naturally or otherwise). In the world of schools and businesses, people have developed a pattern of streamlining the way we find resources and use them. Powerful economic homes, towns, countries, and companies follow the traditional management of resources by buying them. When conventional means do not work, the results often cause frustration and fear. Unlike strong economies, people who have less can do more with less, as was the case in Trinidad. In a stable economic condition, the drum would be bought, but those that have less are put in a position of being resourceful with what they possess. Resource development is dictated by people in different circumstances, situations, and histories. This chapter started with the recollections of Homer Hickam, a young man who went from a very small West Virginia town to become a rocket scientist with NASA. Like the oppressed population of Trinidad, persistence led to success, once again showing that oppression and circumstances out of a person's control do not have to define their success.

(2)

IN 1776, THE FIRST Continental Congress lacked a way to recruit citizens to be soldiers. With the American Revolution underway, human resources were in high demand, and citizens were trained as quickly as possible to be soldiers to defend the newly formed

United States. One recruitment incentive the newly formed Congress developed was a pension program for soldiers that became disabled in the war. For the most part, disabled veterans of the American Revolution were cared for by their local communities and states. In 1811, the federal government authorized the first medical facility specifically for veterans. Then in 1812, the Naval Home in Philadelphia opened as the first facility to provide medical care for veterans. The Civil War would have a significant effect on the growth of the National Home for Disabled Volunteer Soldiers. Though the original proposition for a soldiers' home was to offer a live-in facility, by the 1920s these homes were used with a greater focus on hospital care.

In 1947, there were ninety-seven Veterans Administration (VA) hospitals, which served many men and women. By 1988, the increasing need for veteran hospitals led to President Ronald Reagan signing the Department of Veterans Affairs Act; this took the Veterans Administration to a cabinet level. Today, the VA provides veterans with a wide array of benefits including preventative care, dentistry, immunizations, nutrition, education, physical exams, counseling, and long-term care services. It is a positive program for veterans, but its essential services make it an expensive endeavor. In 2014, there were approximately 21.4 million veterans in the United States. The Department of Veteran Affairs employs 312,841 people to serve the rising number of veterans in 151 medical care centers and 827 outpatient clinics. To run the Department of Veteran Affairs, the 2015 federal government (the taxpayers) paid 163.9 billion dollars. This staggering cost increased by 6.5% from

2014 because veterans are living longer, and the cost of healthcare is rising.

Who will go on paying for the Veterans Administration as its budget continues to swell? The income the federal government has is generated through loans and taxes. The difficulty of an expanding budget is that funds are not infinite. Eventually, there must be a cap. School systems, colleges, towns, states, and households also face this ever-growing concern. Unfortunately, there is a money ceiling.

Since the Industrial Revolution, the United States has experienced a relative steady stream of money rolling in at a regular rate. Though the US has faced a depression and several recessions, when plotted on a graph, the growth of the economy in America has been strong. Money has been an abundant resource. The means to acquire other resources has been to buy them. The most rapid growth the Veterans Administration has seen happened during the Herbert Hoover administration, when Hoover signed an executive order consolidating the Veterans Bureau, the Bureau of Pensions, and the National Homes for the Disabled Volunteer Soldiers into one Veterans Administration. The consolidation created a budget of $786 million, which served 4.6 million veterans. The VA is a classic example of single channel resource management. This means that there is only one course for obtaining resources. In this case, resources are purchased with money.

Even if money grew on trees, there comes a point in time when every leaf will be picked. Then what? As costs expand, limitations grow. If there is no money to pay for goods and services, the results are cuts in services, purchased resources, and employment. Nobody is comfortable when budget cuts happen. For this reason, likened to putting all eggs in one basket, single channel management is risky.

Multichannel resource management is a different way of administering a budget. Bartering, which is mostly seen in so-called "third world countries," is an example of this alternative system of obtaining goods and delivering services. Someone who chooses to barter knows exactly what they want; they may trade money, possessions, or services for that item. There is not one course of action that a barterer uses to possess a service or good. They trade through many means. A typical modern bartering scenario may be the following: the barterer wants to book a party hall for $3,000. They do not have $3,000, but they may be able to lower the cost by offering to paint the outside of the party hall. The party hall agrees, but the barterer needs to buy the paint, rollers, and brushes. The barterer knows that the paint store owner needs logs for his wood burning stove, which the barterer has in abundance. The barterer trades logs for the paint and rollers, then paints the party hall, which pays for its rental. A person practicing single channel resource management would pay for the hall with money. However, a multichannel resource manager knows that there is more than one way to obtain resources and services.

The Veterans Administration has been doing business the same way for years. Is there any other way? History would suggest that the answer is yes. In recent years, the Veterans Administration has needed to become creative in order to continue to provide services for the millions of American veterans. Many veterans require medical services including skilled doctors, nurses, and medical supplies. Veterans were promised this care, so there is an obligation to fulfill this commitment. What if the VA suddenly was run by a barterer? Would providing these services through bartering be possible? A barterer without money will look for a way to reduce the price. One way that they may do this is through experimentation with an adult foster care program. This barterer running a VA clinic may suggest that a willing disabled veteran be placed into foster care, with the foster caregiver being given the training to provide primary medical care.

This concept has been experimented with on a small scale. The "Caregivers and Veterans Omnibus Health Services Act of 2010" was signed into law to explore the potential of an adult foster care program. A family opens its doors to a disabled veteran. The host is given training and financial compensation from the government, but the cost of caring for that individual is much lower than what would be needed to house the veteran at a VA hospital. Currently, the Medical Foster Home Program of the United States Department of Veteran Affairs pairs trained caregivers with veterans. In 2014, over 500 veterans were part of this program. The average cost per veteran was less than half the cost of traditional care. This form of multichannel resource management has the potential to create a widespread reduction in cost, while maintaining the necessary services the veteran requires. When budgets tighten, alternative programs that use their resources need to emerge creatively. If they do not, either people will lose jobs, or the quality of the services will diminish.

As schools, towns, businesses, and governments evolve, the tradition of "buy, buy, buy" will succeed as long as there is money. No matter how successful the organization, all groups go through periods of financial challenge. Having a multichannel mindset allows for the survival of the group.

(3)

KATHRINE SWITZER IS not a household name. However, on the third Thursday of April in 1967, she was on the cover of almost every major newspaper in the country. Different events can have significant ripple effects that have the potential to change mindsets. I enjoy walking the typically calm, southern shoreline of Lake Ontario with my dog. Every once in a while, I am surprised when random waves crash up on the shore only to realize they were created by a boat a mile down the coast. Often waves are felt long after the ship has passed. History mimics a similar pattern. People consider the effect of a historic moment long after that moment has passed. Timeliness and actions were on a collision course for Kathrine Switzer in April of 1967.

In popular sports, record holders, champions, and those who attain distinct achievements are immortalized in film, books, and our minds. Pioneers in more obscure sports tend only to be remembered by the small clique of people following or playing that sport.

In 1967, women were not permitted to register for the Boston Marathon. Today 47% of runners in the Boston Marathon competition are female. Kathrine Switzer ran for the Syracuse Harriers Athletic Club. To downplay her gender, she wrote for the Syracuse University newspaper under the abbreviated name K.V. Switzer. Nowadays, due to its popularity, the Boston Marathon's popularity has forced the Boston Athletic Club to create qualifying times to run in the event, but in 1967 a runner simply needed to register and pay the entrance fee. There was only one stipulation in 1967: the runners had to be male. This is not to say females had not run in the Boston Marathon. Though they were not allowed to officially register, women joined the race as unregistered participants. That is to say, they did not wear bib numbers. Though it violated the rules, Switzer registered for the Boston Marathon under the name K.V. Switzer.

The name was overlooked by race coordinators. At the time, it was unimaginable for a female to dare to register, so the initials were not questioned. Switzer was given the number 261. Decked out in a full cotton sweat suit, it did not take long for Switzer to be recognized by the press and race coordinators. What was a woman doing wearing a bib number? The combination of these two groups, accompanied by timing, set off a media frenzy.

Switzer trained with the Syracuse University men's cross country team because there was no women's program. The year was 1966, which predated Title IX legislation that brought gender equality to athletics by six years. Switzer was coached by Arnie Briggs, a mailman and cross country coach. Briggs had run in fifteen Boston Marathons and was happy to have a female runner in his program. Switzer was the only one.

Arnie was a storyteller, and he enjoyed describing his marathoning experiences. He imparted his accounts so well that one day Switzer decided to run the damn thing. Up to that point, females running long distances was discouraged, not only because running was predominantly a male-dominated sport, but some medical professionals believed that a woman's uterus would fall out of her body if she ran extraordinary distances. Briggs explained to Switzer that "No dame ever ran the Boston Marathon." He told her that if she could prove to him that she could competitively run the marathon distance, he would take her to Boston. Inspired, three weeks later Switzer and Briggs ran the twenty-six miles, plus an extra five. The next day, Arnie Briggs showed up at Switzer's dorm room convinced that she should register for the Boston Marathon. Because of Switzer's amateur status, she filled in her AAU number and sent in three dollars cash, which was the entry fee at the time. Two weeks later, Switzer's 235-pound, nationally recognized hammer throwing boyfriend registered. He was also a linebacker on the university football team. He insisted that if a girl could run a marathon, he did not have to train. Even with that mindset, they would marry years later.

The Boston Marathon is always run on Patriot's Day, the third Monday in April. The weather for the 1967 race was cold and rainy. However, Switzer was from Syracuse, a city familiar with snow. Dressed in a baggy cotton sweat suit, she pinned number 261 to her sweatshirt. As the coach and his young female mentee approached the start, he noticed Switzer was wearing lipstick. As the race started, many of the joggers did double takes as they ran alongside Kathrine Switzer. Yes, she was a female. What were the reactions from the male runners as they realized a female was officially in the race? Surprisingly, most were welcoming. Many asked questions such as, "Will you get my wife to run?" or remarked, "It is great to see a girl here."

The first few miles were uneventful, crowded, and exciting. Most marathons are thick with runners for the first one to two miles until the cluster stretches out. The atmosphere changed when a press bus pulled up next to Switzer. Word had gotten out. A woman was a registered runner in the Boston Marathon. It was exciting to have a moment of recognition but frightening when suddenly a man filled with fury emerged from the bus. That man was coming after Kathrine Switzer. In a Scottish accent, he yelled, "Get the hell out of my race. Give me back my numbers!" referring to the bib. He was a Boston Athletic Association official.

Shortly after that, unprovoked, the man physically attacked Switzer, seeking desperately to rip her numbers from her shirt. Arnie Briggs and Switzer's boyfriend acted, knocking the man off course. The press photographed the entire episode. For a few miles, the official continued cursing at Switzer from the press bus until it ultimately left. When Switzer crossed the finish line in over four hours, she became the first registered female to compete and finish the Boston Marathon. Her time was unimpressive by marathon standards, but her timing was perfect. Pioneering accomplishments cause breakthrough moments when the timing is perfect, on purpose or by total accident.

Some events happen by chance, and some opportunities are

ignored. In 1967 Kathrine Switzer had marathon capability. She would be the "first." The only difference was that Switzer did not realize the full implications of her accomplishment. Even so, Switzer's milestone would change the face of running forever.

Most likely, Kathrine Switzer had no idea that she would be the catalyst to change women's distance running. She merely aspired to rise to a challenge. The timing was coupled with an opportunity, and Switzer had unearthed a gold mine. After running in the Boston Marathon, Switzer slept as she traveled through the night back to Syracuse. She woke up the next day like any other college student, a little sore and stiff, and very unaware. It was not going to be an average day. Switzer was suddenly propelled into the national spotlight for breaking a barrier once thought to be impenetrable.

(4)

SEVERELY WOUNDED SOLDIERS IN the Vietnam battlefield, mountain climbers, and Eastman Kodak have a glue that connects them all. The Eastman Kodak company's role in World War II is well documented. In 1942, the photography giant was awarded the Army-Navy "E" Award. This was an honor presented to a company whose production facilities achieved distinction for making war equipment. Kodak's cutting-edge machinery and film played a significant role in imaging throughout the war.

In the 1940s, Harry Coover was a scientist and developer working for Kodak. During the war he served with a group of engineers developing plastic gun sights. His task was to work with synthetics and adhesives that were part of the manufacturing process on the sights. Coover was experimenting with a family of chemicals called cyanoacrylates, which are fast-acting adhesives. They attach themselves to almost any surface and rapidly form a solid bond. One challenge when working with cyanoacrylates is that they adhere to surfaces too quickly for standard manufacturing. Therefore, they were rarely used because there was no practical use—or so people thought.

Nine years after Coover worked at Kodak, he was designing jet canopies. Jet canopies are exposed to a great deal of heat and stress. Again, Coover was experimenting with cyanoacrylates without success; they were still just too sticky. But Coover was an innovator. Innovators see what is in front of them and adapt that idea or invention to the period that they are living in.

A lack of resources can often cause frustration, and the level of tolerance for failure varies from person to person. While developing gun sights and jet canopies, Coover could have reached a point where his frustration caused him to give up. Cyanoacrylates are unforgiving and frustrating chemicals for anyone to work with. However, Coover was an innovator and timing was on his side. He saw cyanoacrylates for what they were worth. While they are not a suitable adhesive for gun sights or jet canopies, they could have value as a household product. With a bit of tweaking, superglue was born. It was innovations such as Superglue that helped Coover lead Kodak through their golden age in which sales growth increased from 1.8 billion to 2.5 billion dollars per year. Not all of Kodak's success can be attributed to film sales. Coover led Kodak through the use of "programmed innovation," a management methodology that emphasizes research and development.

Thinking within the moment is a vital component of a wartime field medic. One of the frustrations during the Vietnam War was how to deal with battlefield injuries. Soldiers faced many obstacles when attending to wounds. The terrain and battleground were not conducive to quick evacuations of the injured servicemen, so coping with battlefield injuries was a considerable challenge. The warm and tropical climate of Vietnam caused infections to spread rapidly in open wounds, and there was an inability on the battlefield to control bleeding. The body can lose just so much blood before the situation becomes life-threatening. Coover's innovation of Superglue was the ideal solution. Superglue is lightweight and instantly binds skin together. Superglue, the cyanoacrylate meant to be used on gun sights and jet canopies, became a short-term solution to dealing with battlefield injuries. This bonding agent could be utilized to suture wounds, and it saved innumerable lives. In an unexpected turn of events, this bonding agent that was meant originally to improve gun sites was now used to repair war wounds.

Superglue has also aided mountain climbers. One of the most critical parts of the rock climber's body are the fingertips. Rocks are abrasive, and the cold and dry climate of the mountains causes the skin of the fingertips to crack and wear out. Superglue provides a solution. It binds to the surface of the fingertips, allowing the climber to have artificially callused hands.

Harry Coover's early work with cyanoacrylates saw little success, but like all innovators and inventors he had faith that his ideas would become innovations. They are not immune to the frustration that many people feel when their advancement goes unused. However, a persistent inventor like Harry Coover trusts and believes that with some perseverance, he will discover that his inventions, ideas, and creativity will fill a void where resources are lacking. That is the essence of innovation.

(5)

NOBODY LIKES LOSING. However, in sports, the wins, losses, and timing provide concrete data to assess bottom line success. A win is a win, a loss is a loss, and times do not lie. Vision, skills, and resources are indispensable parts of a sports program. A well-executed bunt to move a runner up in a baseball game or a timely block on a running play in football can change outcomes. If all factors for the success of a football team were considered, what would be most important? An argument could be made for a quality stadium, a knowledgeable coach, and skilled players as factors that affect success. If only one had to be chosen, which one supersedes all others for successful achievement?

John McKissick is the retired head football coach of Summerville High School in South Carolina. He coached there for sixty-two years, and never once missed a game. In 2012, McKissick became the first coach in the history of high school football to reach 600 wins. At his retirement, he had amassed 621 victories. To put this in perspective, only one other coach has secured 500 wins, and it took him 61 seasons. McKissick, a World War II paratrooper, entered coaching in 1951. Today, most states limit the number of football contests a high school team can have in a season. On average, a high school team plays nine to ten games per season, so the likelihood of anyone ever surpassing this mark is miniscule to none.

McKissick has ten state championships averaging out to one state title every six years. If you were to hunt for McKissick's autograph on eBay, good luck, because it's not there. But another coach's signed portrait commands a few hundred dollars. That football coach is the University of Alabama's Nick Saban.

In 2007, the University of Alabama made a bold move when they broke boundaries by constructing a coaching contract worth four million dollars per year to hire Nick Saban. Why did they do this? The University of Alabama realized the resource potential of leadership. Like Homer Hickam's teacher, Ms. Riley, Saban is an advocate for his players with high expectations. It is nice to have a great stadium, crisp uniforms, and quality players, but there is a reason why a solid coach commands top dollar. By 2009, after only two seasons, Saban had won a National Championship, and he followed it up with national titles in 2011, 2012, 2015, 2016, and 2017. The university's investment had paid off. Saban's success is even more impressive when you consider that players are recruited and have a maximum eligibility of five years.

Nick Saban and John McKissick have many qualities in common, though it is a big jump to say that the two coaches have the same job. Both McKissick and Saban have a consistent turnover of athletes. Saban has a national spotlight and a much higher salary. McKissick worked for a public high school, and for most of his career only had a local South Carolina spotlight on him. Saban recruits nationally, but McKissick gets the athletes who live in the Summerville school community. Once John McKissick achieved win number 500, he did make national headlines and was featured on ABC News. Top sportscasters such as Bob Costas interviewed him, and his message was consistent and true to a theme. McKissick recognized the significance of athletes striving toward one shared goal. He had a no-cut policy and awarded a jersey to any athlete who was willing to stick with his program and goals. At first glance, a no-cut policy may seem counterproductive to the goal of winning at all costs. McKissick's athletes had to make the decision to push themselves to keep up with the best athletes, or inevitably they realized they could not and stopped playing. This approach built a culture of hard work, which snowballed onto itself. On McKissick's team, the goal was simple: to win. In the locker room of Summerville High School is the Green Wave Pledge which reads: "One Wave, One Heart, One Commitment: To Win." How does this compare to Nick Saban?

Despite these differences, Saban and McKissick are strikingly similar. Neither coach is willing to tolerate obstacles that stand in the way of their intention to win. Does this make Saban or McKissick innovators like Coover, Switzer, or the VA? No. Neither coach has a method no other coach has done before. However, these two coaches need to be coupled with innovators and exceptional teachers like Ms. Riley because they highlight two components that are essential for innovation to lead to success: extraordinary vision and a personal conviction to settle for nothing less than excellence. Saban and McKissick have only one variable that separate them. McKissick gets the players that live locally. Saban recruits nationally. However, they both win. Why? Challenges arise when athletes arrive full of talent but lacking in drive. Saban has the option to judge character as part of the college recruiting process, but McKissick was unique. He simply got handed the next class of high schoolers. As a result, managing his players and getting them to buy into the concept of "enjoying the win" was essential to his success. Goal setting outlines a direction. Whether the path is fruitful or not, it provides a target. If an archer with a bow and arrow is blindfolded and spun, the archer has no idea where the target is. A comparable philosophy is true for goal setting. A target needs to be seen to be hit; conversely, confusion reigns when the target is unclear. Often leaders become so locked in the "get started" mode that they do not communicate their goals. This leads to failure. The link between Saban and McKissick is straightforward. They both have a crystal-clear communication of their goals and the framework to achieve their vision. The statistics prove that this leads to a long-term pattern of success.

## Interview with Ed Buckbee
*July 19, 2018*
*Huntsville, Alabama*

I met Ed Buckbee in July at a German Octoberfest dinner hosted by the United States Rocket Center. We talked for a long time, and I missed the last shuttle back to where I was staying. Kindly, he gave me a ride. Our entire discussion happened at the rocketry center below the large suspended shell of the Saturn V rocket. Buckbee has been associated with the United States space program since the late 1950s. Buckbee began his space career in 1959 when America's first Mercury astronauts were selected. He was present when the Apollo astronauts lifted off for the moon landings. In 1961, Buckbee transferred to the newly formed NASA's Marshall Space Flight Center where he assisted rocket scientist, Wernher von Braun. As a NASA public affairs officer, he worked with all the Mercury, Gemini and Apollo astronauts. In 1970, he was selected by von Braun to be the first director of the United States Space and Rocket Center.

**Albrecht:** Where are you from?
**Buckbee:** I grew up in Romney, West Virginia, about 90 miles outside of Washington, D.C.
**Albrecht:** I know Romney very well.
**Buckbee:** Really?
**Albrecht:** I taught in New Martinsville, West Virginia.

**Buckbee:** I graduated from West Virginia University. I had an ROTC commission. I was commissioned in the United States Army and was sent to Huntsville, Alabama as a missile officer. That was my first job.

**Albrecht:** Was that what you wanted?

**Buckbee:** No, I was a journalism major. I wanted to be involved in writing public affairs and public relations. So, they put me in that job when I came here as a NASA... I left my Army career, resigned my commission, which was a big decision because I wanted to be a career officer forever, but Kennedy just announced at that very year going to the moon. Me and about 13 other officers from the Army resigned our commission and moved to NASA, and went to work for von Braun, the moon landing people. That was the smartest thing I ever did. I never resented it from day one because I was able to join forces with the guys who built the machine right here. In eight years, we went from scratch to landing on the moon surface, and we kicked the Russians' butts. Meanwhile, the Russians were after us, and that is not remembered. They were trying to beat us to the moon, and we just flat beat them to the moon. We landed six times. This rocket went out of Earth's orbit nine times. Nine times this rocket went out of Earth's orbit, and we forget that now. We haven't been out of Earth's orbit since 1972, and it's almost unfortunate to think that we have not gone back. I was here when all that happened. I worked with the Mercury astronauts: Alan Shepherd, Wally Shirah. I was there. I was their PR guy, and so, I was in the middle of all those flights. And, of course, the greatest thing was to see Apollo 11 land successfully for the first time. Nobody thought that we would land the first time. Everybody thought we would have a wave-off, some glitch would happen, and we would have to come back. That thing went so smoothly. Plus, you had Neil Armstrong running the machine, and he by far was the best qualified astronaut selected. Every other astronaut I knew would say, "Neil was the guy." He was the one to be the first to land because he overcame all sorts of things that were going on in the cockpit. The computer, the little dinky one they had was overloading, they just ignored that. He just drove that thing down and landed successfully, and everything worked. That was an amazing event, and America stood up and said, "We have sent our guys to the moon. We brought them back safely, and we're damn proud of it." And, we kicked the Russians' butts. To have all those people at mission control, the average age of people… twenty-six. Twenty-six years of age in Mission Control!

**Albrecht:** Why do you think they were so young?

**Buckbee:** Because nobody told them that they couldn't do it. They were never told you can't do this. There was nothing out there, no other people out there saying, "Go, go, go, go," except von Braun. I worked for him for fifteen years, and he was an amazing guy. He was very talented in terms of technology-wise, in terms of rocketry, but he understood human beings better than anyone I have ever been around. He could see in a team of people that they could perform, and if they were given the proper tools and support, they could make it happen. He was the leader of our rocket team, and I'll tell ya, the Germans taught us a hell of a lot about how to get things accomplished in technology. This thing right here (the Saturn V), nobody's ever come up with a machine like that, never, and it's been since 1972 since we flew it. We haven't come up with anything like it since 1972. We haven't been out of Earth's orbit since 1972. It's crazy! This country should be on Mars by now, but political decisions were made. Von Braun basically said that after the moon landing, we aren't going to do anything else. They shut that down. The program was completely terminated. Von Braun and the team were ready to go to Mars. He had it worked out in 1982 that we are going to land on Mars… this vehicle with a nuclear upper stage. We would not ignite the nuclear until out of Earth's orbit. This vehicle would put the crew up in Earth's orbit. It would have a nuclear engine. Seven months later they would be on Mars. Two ships, flying side by side. In case one failed, the crew would transfer over to the other. The backup system, everything was all worked out. Nixon killed it. From then on, there was no ability to get back into the space business. So, we waited until the shuttle came along. Of course, the shuttle did a wonderful job getting the International Space Station up there. Basically, it was a freight vehicle, and we got a lot accomplished with the International Space Station, which is still functioning today. Now we have not been out of Earth's orbit since 1972. It's crazy. We're the only country that's been out of Earth's orbit, and we stopped because we did it. So, we need to get back in that. Your generation needs to take that on, and I think it will happen. With the right kind of leadership… I don't think we got it today, but surely someone will come along and recognize the talent in this country. It's still here. I see it in young people. Don't you agree?

**Albrecht:** Oh yes. I sat in on a presentation with an astronaut from STS 50, and their questions were articulate and had serious inquiry. That to me says there is hope.

**Buckbee:** Two things are important in this country: teachers because they teach. Engineers because they create. We've got to keep that alive.

**Albrecht:** So, here's the question. First off, how old are you?

**Buckbee:** I'm 81.

**Albrecht:** You're 81? You look great for 81 years old! OK, 81 years of life, who would you say is your favorite teacher, the most influential?

**Buckbee:** I have to say, it's a journalism teacher I had at West Virginia University. The problem now is I can't think of his name, but I can see his face. He basically was the guy who woke up every day and said, "We put out the newspaper, four days a week." And, we worked on the newspaper. He was our professor who monitored our activities and made sure the paper got out. And, he was the guy that said, "Don't look back. Look to the future, realize that there is talent in this room, and you can deliver the news to Mr. and Mrs. America every day. All you have to do is do your job. And, look, America is a country of freedom, and your mind can be expanded. There is no limit to what you can do in this country." I did not really get a lot of talks about rocketry in a journalism class, but he taught me that communication is important, and you got to continue to inform the public of what you're doing, whether you're in a football game or you're going out and developing a new car or rocket. You gotta understand that Mr. and Mrs. America are supporting that. And, the country will stand up and support you. But, you've got to give them a goal. You've got to challenge them, and I remember, he kept saying that, "You got to be challenged. In this country, if you're not challenged, we don't produce well." And, I think he's right, and Kennedy recognized that. Kennedy recognized something that we didn't know we had, and he stood up and said we are going to the moon in a decade. I remember that I looked around at my buddies and said, "Hey, we got a damn job now." We were right here at that time. I was twenty-three years old, and all of the sudden, Kennedy challenged us to build this moon rocket, and we never went to bed for days. I'm serious. It was like, we have a goal. We had a challenge, and we would produce. It was a great time to live from '61 to '69. It was a special time for us, my generation, anyway. We got all the money we needed. We got all the support we needed. This guy, von Braun, I wish you could have met him. You talk about an unbelievable, futuristic thinking guy. Ya know, he designed this rocket. Nobody's ever duplicated this rocket. Ever! A bunch of people have tried. Everybody's tried. We were fortunate to have the Germans come to this part of the country. One hundred-twenty of them came here, and I worked with them for twenty years. Then, he and I built this museum. He was the one who came up with this idea to build a museum, not me. And, Space Camp was also his idea.

**Albrecht:** Werhner von Braun's idea?

**Buckbee:** Yeah.

**Albrecht:** Really…

**Buckbee:** He believed you had to show the public what you were doing. You don't do it, hide it, and cover it up. You put it out and let the public see it. He was a teacher in another form, and he shared it with the American public. Fun guy to work for. Always looking to the future. Never satisfied with what we are doing today. So, we had a lot of fun.

Most of us were wearing Army uniforms. And, Kennedy came along and said, "We're going to have a space agency." And, basically, we evacuated from the Army and moved across the street. Von Braun headed up this thing called the Marshall Space Flight Center. Seven thousand of us became part of the Marshall Space Flight Center. That is when they started building these rockets. He was the guy that convinced us that we could go to the moon. Astronauts came here. Mercury astronauts were friends of ours. Alan Shepard, Wally Shirah, John Glenn, and all of those guys...

**Albrecht:** You knew all of them?

**Buckbee:** I did. I managed their public relations for three years. I was the guy who kinda created and managed where they went. Then when they were retired, they came here and helped me with Space Camp. Shepard believed in Space Camp.

**Albrecht:** Really!?!

**Buckbee:** Yeah, he and Wally Shirah believed that we needed to have another generation of astronauts. Shepard, of course, said, "I know what you're doing Buckbee. You're creating little Alan Shepards for the future." He couldn't resist saying stuff like that. He was that kind of a guy. But, they loved Space Camp. They really did because they saw in those young people the same thing that was in their mind and their thinking pattern because they were given an opportunity to step up into a whole new world. We were doing the same thing at Space Camp at an early age. So, that's why they liked it. I think they really supported it because they could see themselves in that little kid out there running around and playing astronaut. When I started, I thought it basically will be a local thing. When "Space Camp" the movie came out, it was like a commercial. We had to almost shut the door when the movie came out. It just created a whole new world of interest, and it has been going strong ever since. I think they have had 800,000 kids go through Space Camp from all over the world, and it's growing, growing, growing. Well, and the other thing too that I recognize is the parents that bring their kids here are committed. There are certain parents that pay attention to what that kid wants to do, what he thinks he should be doing, and giving him the proper exposure as he develops. It's their investment. I'm impressed on graduation day when the parents come to pick up their kid. You can see they're happy about the kid's interest, what he's shown by going through Space Camp. It's reaching our kids at this age bracket, and it's good it's continuing. I was afraid it was going to burn out. It would start, and in about three or four years, it would burn out. But, it's grown and is more popular now, which is a good sign.

## Reflection:

Over 18 months, I interviewed anyone who was willing. The number of interviews was in the hundreds, and with the high number of people, I was not surprised that patterns emerged. One phenomenon is the role that age has with what the interviewee values. Almost every time I interviewed a person over fifty years of age, they identified a teacher with a cognitive skill set. There was an appreciation of what that teacher knew or the skills they possessed. Formal education was highly valued. When I interviewed a person under 40, they nearly always recalled a teacher who had an impact on his or her social and emotional development. Ed Buckbee was 81 at the time of this interview, and his response and narrative about early development classically fell in line with the way many people of his age answered. Buckbee's favorite teacher remained nameless because he could not recall his name. However, he did recall the work ethic and professionalism that his journalism teacher instilled in him. Buckbee valued his skill set and knowledge.

Ed Buckbee is the oldest person interviewed that I included in this book. Though there were outliers, most people over the age of fifty acknowledged and valued teachers for their skill set, knowledge and discipline. People that I interviewed under the age of forty gravitated toward educators who developed social-emotional relationships with them. Admittedly, there were outliers, but generally, this was a pattern. Though this book does not answer why this phenomenon exists, there is a pattern. It is a compelling subject to explore. The phenomena sheds light on many questions. Has the value system changed in schools? Did teachers keep a greater emotional distance years ago? Or do we look back on our educational experience with a different lens as we age?

Ed Buckbee's interview contains a rich account of what it was like to be in the thick of the action at NASA, beginning with the Mercury missions. He witnessed iconic events firsthand and most likely has told about many of the moments in this interview thousands of times. When I interviewed him, it was like he had held the story in for decades just waiting to tell somebody. Though Buckbee cited a journalism teacher at the University of West Virginia as his favorite educator, this interview illustrates the depth and lasting effect of a mentor. Dr. Werhner von Braun mentored Buckbee for more than two decades, and together they created Space Camp. Space Camp is a world-class destination for children, teens, and adults located at the United States Space and Rocket Center in Huntsville, Alabama. As of 2018, over 800,000 people have attended Space Camp since it was first opened in 1982. Though a mentor may not be the first person that comes to mind when a person is asked about their favorite teacher, mentors are indeed educators.

I write many messages to my students. I communicate every week in my college students' journals and spend hours leaving notes in my fourth graders' lockers and on their assignments. I give a lot of written feedback. Often, I close a note with "Your Friend, Christopher Albrecht." Mentorship, friendship, and student-teacher relationships do not have clear lines. Can a student also be a friend? There is a gray area here.

What is the line dividing a teacher and a friend? Teachers are adults, and students are children or adolescents. At the college level, students are older, but they still are students. Most of a teacher's thoughts do not match where our students are at in their development. However, nine-year-old students grow up to become adults and, if a teacher is fortunate, friends. What obligation do teachers have after a student is no longer in their classroom? I would argue that once a person formally or informally takes on the role of being a teacher to a student, that mentor has a lifelong commitment and responsibility to always be that student's teacher. Lucky and committed teachers grow old enough to have some of their students become their friends.

When students look back on a grade level, there is a close bond and enduring memory of a teacher. All teachers need to be aware that they may have left a permanent imprint on the souls of their students. This cannot be taken lightly. There may be moments, positive or negative, when a student comes back. Teaching is a unique profession. If we are going to make differences in people's lives, we must be committed for life. The oldest person I have interviewed was ninety-four at the time of the interview. She recalled a chorus teacher who instructed her for one hour per week during her sophomore year. A typical school year runs about forty weeks. Adding in time at concerts, that woman may have spent only sixty hours with that teacher, yet eighty years later, she is still affected by the impact of those precious hours.

Ben is a United States Marine, but for two years, he was my fourth and fifth grade student. I remain in contact with him. He graduated and entered the Marines. We talk by phone or visit when he comes home. He asks questions, and usually, I do too. He still calls me Mr. Albrecht, so there will always be a student-teacher bond, but Ben is a grown man now. Is he a friend? Absolutely, but with an asterisk. We can share adult conversation now, but I believe that I will always represent a teacher to him, and though I see a man when we get together, there are memories of a boy in my classroom that are there too. We cannot erase memories. No matter their ages or the amount of time that has passed, teachers will always see their former students as students, and former teachers will be teachers.

Ed Buckbee's recollection of Werhner von Braun reminds me a lot of how I would describe my relationship with Ben. We have adult conversations, but there is a difference between our friendship and that of my closest friend, Jeff. Jeff and I grew up together. I would assume Buckbee's view of Werhner von Braun is like Ben's view of me. Buckbee describes von Braun as this "futuristic guy," and says that, "I wish you could have met him". He credits von Braun for the vision to create Space Camp. That may be true, but von Braun empowered Buckbee to become the first director of Space Camp. Von Braun was in charge, and Buckbee worked for him. There was a friendship, but also there was a relationship like a teacher and a student.

# Chapter 5
## What Alan Shepard Discovered the Night Before the Launch

(1)

A JUVENILE IS STANDING in front of a glass wall. On the opposite side of the wall is candy. The child is quite young, but not so naive that he does not recognize what candy is. To get to the candy, the child first pushes on the glass wall. The glass is thick and much too strong to shatter. Like any child, he tries climbing, but the barrier is much too tall. As a last effort, the child attempts to dig beneath the wall, but the ground is too solid. With every creative idea, the child fails to seize the candy on the other side of the wall. With tears and frustration, the child walks to their right, and to his surprise, he finds that he can walk around the wall. Quickly the child runs to the candy.

The next day arrives, and the same child is placed in front of the glass wall. There is candy on the other side of the

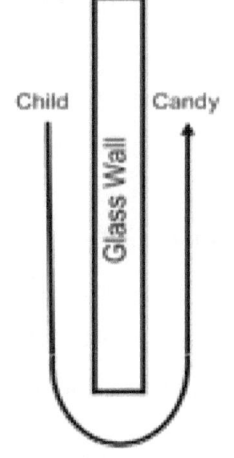

wall. Does the child try to push through, climb over, or dig under the wall? Of course not. After failures from the day before, the child has learned to walk around the wall. If this study is replicated day after day, it is plausible that the child will continue to follow this pattern. The child made an accidental discovery. Even if one day the wall is opaque, that child, after being patterned day after day, will most likely go around the wall.

In its most elementary form, seizing the candy is a metaphor for the attainment of success and achievement. Was the child successful when trying to go over, under, or through the wall? No. Once that child found success, his behavior replicated itself time after time. That child understood he had found the key to success and most likely will never deviate from his pattern. For a century, Kodak was following a pattern similar to the child. Like the child, the company discovered a path to success. Metaphorically, they walked around the wall to attain their success for many years. Their progress, profit, and success were generated in large quantities from film production, and the manufacturing of film was their lifeblood with relatively little change up until the 1990s. Advancements in film size and quality changed somewhat, but the fundamental system of exposing film to light through a shutter remained nearly unchanged. For decades, Kodak came to the glass wall, turned right, and walked around the wall to reach success.

In the second picture, when the child turns right, he has to walk quite a distance to go around the wall. Why would the child continue this pattern? Each time he turns right, the move leads him to success. Once he knows he will reach success, will he think to try anything else? If the child would only turn left, he would have a shorter path to the candy. Why does he never consider going this way? He knows that the turn to the right will always lead to candy, so why would he change? Success sometimes causes blindness to creativity. This is very dangerous. In all walks of life, when people stop investing in creativity, they will hit a wall and lose their competitive edge. When people, corporations, schools, governments, or families fall into patterns where they get too comfortable with success, work ethic and creativity diminish. Safeguards must be put in place that force people to challenge themselves during times of success. These measures force us to always look to the left.

Donatella Versace is a fashion icon recognized worldwide. She is the youngest of four children whose father established the Versace fashion dynasty. Her clothing, accessories, and styles distinctively develop and change from year to year. How has she not fallen into the pattern of always turning right? Her net worth is over 200 million dollars. She owns 20% of the Versace Group, whose lavish runway shows attract the attendance of Sir Elton John, Katherine Zeta-Jones, and Prince Charles. Versace has said, "Creativity comes from a conflict of ideas." It can be inferred that Versace is implying that the opposition of ideas and the actions that go with them cause success. The child seeking candy had no conflict of ideas. Day after day, he walked around the glass wall, always turning to the right because he knew that, in the end, it would lead to success. There is no conflict because there is no need for conflict. What would happen if one day, after fifty years of going the same way for the same treat, it was not there? Without even glancing through the glass wall, the person who has done the same routine for fifty years suddenly discovers there is nothing behind the wall. Initially, confusion would occur, presumably followed by frustration, and then ultimately panic. Think back to what Versace said: a conflict of ideas. What if, from the inception of the experiment, the glass wall was altered every day? This would have to be a conscious act. Initially, this would cause discomfort. Some days the treat would be placed at the end of the wall, that is, to the very far left. Would this "conflict of ideas" cause creativity to emerge in the individual's mind? By creating a conflict of ideas, we are, for the most part, not allowing success to stifle creativity. Changes in the patterns of the way that people live their lives allow for creativity to flourish.

If we "move the candy" regularly, the thought process that defines success has to morph as well. Creativity is a craft that needs to be exercised and practiced daily. We are born and go through childhood with it. If we are fortunate, we experience a life of fulfillment in which we retain it.

Infused creativity in times of success needs to start in homes and schools at the earliest of ages, so that it becomes second nature as a person grows. If this is accomplished, then the child grows to be accustomed to automatically looking for creative ways to solve problems. After years of practice, the individual will have practiced the management of their frustration level, and slowly other individuals can be introduced. If they are coached to communicate and solve problems collectively, they will understand that the collection of many people's thoughts is far more valuable and effective than one. In the end, those students will understand how to peacefully work together to solve the complex and ever-changing challenges of the world. They will have greater resilience and will be successful.

(2)

ALEX OSBORN LIVED from 1888 to 1966. It is common for most people to reach the pinnacle of their careers in their 40s and 50s. For Osborn, his highest earning potential was during America's most significant financial crisis, the Great Depression. Nevertheless, he is credited for using a uniquely creative approach in the advertising business. This method saved corporate giants such as General Electric, Chrysler, Royal Crown Cola, American Tobacco, BF Goodrich, and Du Pont from economic ruin. How did he do it? The answer is simple: creative advertising. Advertising prior to the 1940s was mostly limited to statements about what a product did. In 1942, Osborn published a groundbreaking novel called *How to Think Up*. In this book, he coined a new technique for generating creative ideas: brainstorming.

Osborn was from Buffalo, New York. After retiring from the business of advertising, he teamed up with Sydney Parnes, a professor at Buffalo State College, to create a structured process for brainstorming called Creative Problem Solving (CPS). It was so successful that Buffalo State College began offering advanced degrees in creativity. After a few years, the instructors and participants in the program developed a group called the Creative Education Foundation. Its mission was "to engage and develop the next generation of creative thinkers and innovators." The more ideas that were shared, the more potential there was for creative advancement. However, the distribution of ideas had its flaws as well.

In elementary school, many people first experience brainstorming as part of the writing process. Brainstorming happens when people get into a cohort. The group is presented with a predicament, an idea, or a prompt. During brainstorming, the group appoints a scribe or recorder to document all ideas generated by members of the group, no matter how far-fetched those ideas are. By sharing without limitations, no matter how implausible an idea or thought is, the proposal is validated by recording it on the chart of ideas. Though brainstorming is widely used in schools, its earliest roots grew in the advertising business.

Brainstorming often works well for generating original and creative ideas, but is there a better means to enhance creativity? Tens of thousands of classrooms around the world start the writing process, scientific investigations, and even mathematical computations with the process of brainstorming. To argue against the tradition of brainstorming is to oppose a broadly used and accepted form of generating ideas.

Great ideas have their critics. Grassroots brainstorming, at its core, requires collaboration. Most of the time, this is done through conversations. Some people do not mind advocating for their thoughts, and some people prefer to argue to see other's reactions. People who feel comfort within verbal communication are born to brainstorm. Though some individuals love sharing ideas, and others enjoy listening, there are others who have to force themselves to remember not to talk over other people's ideas. Fortunately, not every person is forceful with their thoughts, or the world would be full of explosive conversations. There are those who blush in the face of opposition.

Conventional brainstorming challenges people to communicate. Each person is unique, and speaking in groups is not something that all people are comfortable with. Nearly all scientific research on introverted and extroverted people find it inconclusive that these two groups are any more or less intelligent than each other. Microsoft founder, Bill Gates, is not only a fluent and talented public speaker, but he is also an extrovert. He is confident in front of audiences and adversaries, and he offers his ideas and opinions, whether he is asked or not. Gates is a very successful humanitarian, entrepreneur, philanthropist, and husband. In contrast is Apple co-founder, Steve Wozniak, who single-handedly designed the Apple I and Apple II computers in the later part of the 1970s. Wozniak prefers to draw his energy by working in intimate settings out of the spotlight. Steve Jobs took Wozniak's ideas and convinced him they could be marketed and sold. Wozniak once said, "Most inventors and engineers are like me. They are shy, and they live in their heads. The very best of them are artists, and artists work best alone."

In Ed Buckbee's interview, he talked a lot about Wernher von Braun's outstanding ability to communicate. Of von Braun he stated, "He understood humans better than anyone I have ever known." Surely, von Braun's group of seven thousand scientists at Marshall Space Center were not only talented, but diverse in personalities. Von Braun understood that successful teamwork and brainstorming would occur when groups were well-rounded. All members of the group were versed in contributing to what they were working on and listened well to their peers.

Introverts and extroverts are equally capable of success. Within a random group of people, most research suggests that one third to one half of the group will be introverted. This statistic is supported by Susan Cain, a former Wall Street lawyer and author of the TED Talk "The Power of Introverts." Cain states that there is a distinction between a person being shy and being an introvert. A shy person fears social judgment. This is not the mindset of an introvert, who responds to social stimulation differently. Extroverts create much social stimulation, but an introvert feels alive in quieter environments. Therefore, introverts seem shy even though many are not. An introvert struggles to be at their peak of performance when there is lively stimulation.

When it comes to sharing time, whose voice do you think will be heard: the extrovert's or the introvert's? There is a flaw that most opponents to brainstorming point out. Brainstorming is an attractive venue for the extroverted, but what about those who are less inclined to share? What if brainstorming was the only way for Steve Wozniak to produce work, and he did not have the natural drive to share his brilliant inventions? It is feasible to conclude that there would not be any Apple computers.

How do you get people who are introverted to come forward and share what is on their mind? To keep progress moving, it is essential that all people are part of the brainstorming process.

(3)

GREAT IDEAS MUST be shared, but what if a person for one reason or another does not want to do so? Introversion may initially be a hindrance in leadership. It is a misconception that introverts do not like to be around people and would rather spend most of their time alone. The central difference between extroverts and introverts is how they "charge their internal batteries." Extroverts amass their energy through social situations. By comparison, introverts recharge through quiet solitude and contemplation. Excessive stimulation drains an introvert. It is rather ambiguous. We think of leaders as confident, outgoing, and in some cases, willing to voice unpopular ideas. Vision, work ethic, process-oriented mindsets, timing, resourcefulness, and public perception are several key factors that increase the possibility of success. Are these skills manipulated and possessed only by extroverts?

There seems to be a natural human inclination to first gravitate toward an extrovert when choosing a leader. Most extroverts have charisma, and in the brief window during a decision-making period, they tend to capture the moment. Charisma persuades people, and this can overshadow quieter, more reflective people. The effect of persuasion due to quick decisions based on the allure of one person can lead to huge mistakes. Introverts, given time, may even outshine their extroverted counterparts.

Adam Grant is a psychologist at the University of Pennsylvania. In 2011, Grant published a study regarding fifty-seven store managers from a nationally recognized pizza chain. The core of Grant's investigation was to identify what all companies want to know: What type of leadership does the business world require to increase the bottom line? Grant and his colleagues discovered that when employees were empowered to take more significant initiative and act proactively upon suggestions made by a manager, profits increased. Interestingly, stores managed by introverts saw profits rise 14% higher than stores led by extroverts. To ensure that his findings were accurate, Grant repeated the research using college students with a different scenario. Participants were asked to fold t-shirts for ten minutes. Participants were randomly grouped and told if they were the most successful, they would be rewarded with an iPod Nano. Groups managed by introverts who acted proactively saw a 28% increase in production. The parallel linking these two studies shows that introverted people can produce both long- and short-term success. Therefore, it is a misconception that introverts are shy. Introverts are reflective listeners.

In the practice of healthcare, is it more beneficial for a physician to be extroverted or introverted? Though introverts are initially more reflective, the t-shirt study does confirm that introverts can make immediate and successful decisions. Introverts may not have the pleasant bedside manner of extroverts, but when making a decision concerning health, introverts may be a sound bet. Introverts, on average, listen more. By listening, the chance that small changes in health data or a patient's subtle comments heard goes up. The contemplative nature of an introvert also lends itself more naturally toward self-directed leadership.

Jeffrey Alan Gray, a British psychologist, spent a significant portion of his career clarifying personality types. In the mid-20th century, he developed a personality psyche called the "Big Five." Gray saw dispositions as contracting behaviors. Here is his list:

- Openness to Experience (inventive/curious vs. consistent/cautious)
- Conscientiousness (efficient/organized vs. easy-going/careless)
- Extroversion (outgoing/energetic vs. solitary/reserved)
- Agreeableness (friendly/compassionate vs. analytical/detached)
- Neuroticism (sensitive/nervous vs. secure/confident)

People can have combinations of the "Big Five." Some of the descriptive words that illustrate the five personalities are not considered favorable in today's world. For example, the words careless, detached, and nervous carry negative connotations, while the traits of energetic, outgoing, and curious sound quite positive. However, each trait can become extremely important if the right state of affairs dictates its need.

Different circumstances lend themselves to various leaders with different traits. Therefore, a balance needs to be made in which an environment is created for multiple leaders to share ideas with varied skill sets. This is a typical situation I often have in the college class I instruct. A group of graduate students needs to develop a presentation together. Most groups have a variety of personalities. How does a timid member of a group contribute? If nerves are channeled correctly, it is likely that student will be watching for the small subtleties such as punctuation and spelling, using accurate citations, and so on. These details are generally overlooked by people that Gray would refer to as easy-going and careless. Well-rounded groups are conscientious about making sure that all people's skill sets are considered to produce extraordinary results. When von Braun assembled teams to work on projects, surely he was keenly aware of the importance of diversifying the participants, even by personality types.

In the pizza manager study, introverted managers succeeded more than those that were extroverted. Why? Initially, their first course of action was to reflect. Introverted managers saw the strengths within each of their employees. They did not immediately dictate a direction and therefore empowered their crew.

In 2012 Susan Cain authored the book *Quiet: The Power of Introverts in a World That Can't Stop Talking*. Her book highlighted the sentiment that certain cultures, especially Western ones, do not embrace the ability and importance of introverted people. In short, a squeaky wheel gets the oil. Consider workplaces. Very few jobs do not involve some form of teamwork. Schools have grown more collaborative. Cain points out that traditional schools had desks in rows. Students tended to work in isolation. There were periods of silence where children had to explore their minds to create, solve problems, and understand. What do classrooms look like today? For the most part, desks are connected in clusters or islands to put students in a collaborative forum.

Classrooms have a mix of many people with many dispositions who prefer varying degrees of participation. Some students are naturally bold and impulsively talk. If the student does not control this impulse at the correct time during instruction, he gets into trouble. By comparison, if a student is quiet by nature, he never or rarely gets into trouble by staying quiet; this means that traditional schools allow for most introverts to go about their day comfortably. Historically, most conventional schooling, jobs, cottage industries, and trades did not require significant collaboration. The information era has increased the number of ways that people can connect. Walls in offices have been torn down. Projects are collaborative, and desks are clustered together. The world we now live in, by design, is made for the extroverts. Extroverts do contribute, but based on research, there are many introverts in the world. Some notable names include Michael Jordan, Barack Obama, and Steven Spielberg. Each person has been successful in a collaborative world, but their nature is to recharge their internal batteries in quiet and around few to no people.

Is it possible for introverted leaders to rise to the top? Thomas Jefferson was born in 1743. Documentation indicates that he was introverted, though he likely would not have used that term. Consider Jefferson's accomplishments. He not only was the author of the Declaration of Independence, but he held leadership positions, including Governor of Virginia, third President of the United States, and Foreign Minister to France. Jefferson was a linguist, inventor, architect, and founder of the University of Virginia. Most documentation of the third president indicates that he was quiet and avoided speaking in public. Many people described Jefferson as emotionally cold; however, in small groups, he was sympathetic and led intense conversations.

Richard Nixon was also a confirmed introvert. Nixon had a

considerable capacity to read and comprehend complex information and literature. He often retreated to his room and wrote in longhand on legal paper. Calvin Coolidge once said, "Don't you know that four-fifths of all of the troubles in this life would disappear if we would just sit down and keep still?" No doubt this is a sage quote from a classic introverted leader.

(4)

ERNAKULAM IS IN the eastern mainland portion of the city of Kochi in Kerala, India. It is home to over 3.3 million citizens in a bustling urban setting. This population has increased significantly from just 21,901 people in 1911. Kochi gets drenched during the monsoon season and bakes in the tropical heat of summer. Its economy relies on shipbuilding, technology, and tourism. People from all over the world travel to Ernakulam to visit its old temples and churches and experience the rich history of this ancient land.

India's women have fought a centuries-old uphill battle for equality. Though women have occupied the offices of President, Prime Minister, Governor, Chief Minister, and Union Minister, full equality is not a reality in India. The Indian constitution guarantees that women should receive equal opportunities, equal pay, and the same dignity as men, but according to a Reuters report, among the twenty strongest economies in the world, India ranks last for women's safety. India is making progress, but change is slow.

Kudumbashree is a program which started in 1998 with just a few thousand women. Its concentrated focus is on the empowerment of women by providing low cost loans to create businesses. Many of the women do not have the money to start a business. Some examples of startups include small companies that produce handmade crafts, schools, paper mills, taxi services, and farms. Until the start of Kudumbashree, working women remained a moderately untapped resource. The United Nations Development Program has recognized the program's success as one of the twenty best practices in India. Two critical components of Kudumbashree stimulate its progressive success and growth. First, female business owners are fully empowered. Because the program started with a few thousand women, the odds are that all of the personality profiles outlined by Jeffery Gray are all represented many times over by the first women who pioneered this program. The group designates its leaders, which allows for all constructs of personalities to contribute. Secondly, the system is operated as a commune. Regular meetings of a governance board oversee profitability. Unsuccessful businesses are closed. There is a balance between independence and accountability. Because women work in a cooperative, they sustain success, even when a single venture fails. The result of the empowerment of the women of the Kudumbashree has had a snowball effect; in 2010, 11,000 Kudumbashree women ran for public office. Half of them won. This has led to improvements in education, healthcare, and insurance for millions of families.

Today 3.7 million women are members of Kudumbashree. The continued success has grown from the once-silenced and oppressed voices and ideas of women. Silence and oppression are factors that cause people to be overlooked, and their ideas fail to get shared. However, when that once-silenced voice is empowered, success often comes with it.

(5)

OPERATION PAPERCLIP WAS the code name that the United States military used post-WWII, after the fall of Germany, on a high stakes game of scientific tug of war. The V-2 rocket was the world's first long range ballistic missile that could be guided. This rocket was developed by German scientists. It allowed them to retaliate and attack at a 200-mile range, an incredible advancement at the time. On June 20th, 1944, the V-2 rocket became the first entity made by human hands to travel into space. More valuable than the V-2 rocket technology were the scientists that were developing it. When World War II ended early in September of 1945, a high-stakes tug was on between the United States and the Soviet Union to get the scientists who developed the technology of rocketry. The US and the Soviets were entrenched in the Cold War Era, and advancements in rocket technology were in high demand.

The German scientists had a decision to make. Under Operation Paperclip, the United States Army convinced over 1,600 German scientists, technicians, and engineers to come work and live in the United States. The Soviets exerted a much firmer approach by taking an estimated 2,200 people from the German rocketry community, many at gunpoint. The United States and the Soviet Union recognized that the technology these scientists understood would provide their nation with the upper hand in the arms race. The scientists had the intellect to help advance military power and provide a considerable momentum for the progress of rocket expertise. These German scientists' technology could have the potential to propel either country ahead in a race to launch satellites and, eventually, humans into space. As a young 34-year-old scientist, Wernher von Braun came to the United States as one of the most respected scientists under Operation Paperclip.

Ed Buckbee was born just before World War II, and in 1958, as a new journalism graduate of West Virginia University and Potomac State College, he began a career with the United States Army Ballistic Missile Program. Progress in rocketry development was deverloping at a rapid pace and the timing could not have been better for Buckbee. His job was to chronicle the advancements of rocket technology, which allowed him to work closely with Wernher von Braun and many of the scientists. Buckbee would witness unbelievable developments as the United States worked toward President Kennedy's objective of landing a man on the moon. His timing and job provided him with a unique first-hand vantage point to witness some of the most iconic moments in NASA's history. In 1970, Wernher von Braun would give Buckbee his full support to become the first Director of the United States Space and Rocketry Center in Huntsville, Alabama. There he would assemble the world's most extensive collection of rocketry equipment and historical artifacts. The center opened a space camp, where children and adults from all over the world could come to learn about space and the new frontiers of space technology.

By nature, successful people attract other successful people. Ed Buckbee had access to the finest astronauts and scientists during the late 1950s, 60s, and 70s. As a trained journalist, he presented their stories to the world. Buckbee spent time with America's first astronaut, Alan Shepard. Shepard would be the second person in human history to go into space, and he would travel to the moon aboard Apollo 14.

As told by Ed Buckbee, on the night of January 30th, 1971, Alan Shepard could not sleep. Apollo 14 was scheduled for its flight to the moon the next day. Like a quarterback walking to midfield in an empty stadium before a big game, Shepard got into his pickup truck and drove to the Florida launch pad at the Kennedy Space Center.

Shepard was the commander of this space mission. He had come back from incredible odds that should have permanently sidelined him from ever again going into space. Shepard was suffering dizzy spells that began in 1963, and this grounded him from flight. His condition turned out to be an inner ear disorder called Ménière's disease, which causes vertigo and ringing in the ears. Fortunately, a procedure was developed and successfully performed to correct the problem. Once he recovered, he was eligible to go into space again. Shepard was the first American to go into space, but arguably could have been the first human in space had delays not happened in the United States space program. It must have eaten away at Shepard to know that the United States had the technology to put him in space first, but delays allowed the Soviet astronaut, Yuri Gagarin, to beat him to it.

Shepard was committed to do everything he could to get himself personally onto the surface of the moon. Gordon Cooper, the backup commander for Apollo 10, did not share Shepard's commitment, and the people at NASA sensed it. Shortly after the Apollo 12 mission, Shepard replaced Cooper. Originally, Shepard was supposed to command Apollo 13, but to allow for adequate training, he was moved to Apollo 14.

Alone in his pickup truck, Shepard arrived at the rocket the night before the launch. He took the elevator up the 363-foot-tall Saturn V rocket. About halfway up, Shepard noticed a light emanating from inside of the rocket. He stuck his head in the door to find an engineer. This was hours before the mission.

After a quick hello, he said to the engineer, "I guess you know how this whole rocket works?"

The man responded, "No sir, I don't, but I'm here tonight to make sure my part does!" The words of this one engineer reflected not only his feelings, but the feelings of all the engineers working on the Apollo mission. To ensure success, every person who is part of a team must understand that they play a critical role. The history books will record Alan Shepard and his journey to the moon, but what if that engineer failed to make sure his part worked perfectly? The hundreds of millions of people that work quietly behind the scenes for those who make it into the headlines are vital to the success of any endeavor. Apple grew out of a garage in the 1970s to become a computer and technology icon. How many hours did Steve Wozniak spend in a garage engineering early Apple computers out of the public eye? Most likely he devoted just as much time as that engineer in the rocket.

Ed Buckbee presents often, and when he tells the story about

Alan Shepard and the engineer, he ends his talk with, "Yes, ladies and gentlemen, that's how we got to the moon. Over 400,000 Americans made sure their part worked."

# Interview with Stephen Duckworth
*July 24, 2018*
*Huntsville, Alabama*

Stephen Duckworth's classroom was three doors down from my first classroom. He was my mentor during the first three years of my teaching career. Duckworth is a retired art teacher. He spent nearly all of his life teaching in West Virginia before retiring to Alabama. This interview was done at a coffee shop.

**Albrecht:** I'm with…

**Duckworth:** Stephen Duckworth.

**Albrecht:** Steve, you started teaching in Fairmont, West Virginia. Is that correct?

**Duckworth:** Yes, that's correct.

**Albrecht:** So, what is your background? Where were you born?

**Duckworth:** I was born in Elkins, which is in West Virginia. It is a mountain town, and I was raised near Clarksburg, out in the country. It was called Parker Hill. I went to a one room school.

**Albrecht:** What was the name of the school?

**Duckworth:** Parker Hill School. I went to a one room school until I was in the 6th grade. Then schools were consolidated, and I went to a middle school, Monongah Middle School. I continued there to Monongah High School, and then received a scholarship and finished my education at Fairmont State College with a degree in education. I went to Marshall for my masters. So, I'm a graduate of Fairmont State and Marshall University.

**Albrecht:** And how old are you?

**Duckworth:** I turned 70 four days ago.

**Albrecht:** Well, happy birthday. So, I am going to ask you one question. First, that one room schoolhouse, was it first grade through sixth grade?

**Duckworth:** It was actually first grade through eighth grade. We had students who lived in the country who actually didn't go beyond the eighth grade, but they stayed in school. There was one student who was handicap, and he went to school until he was 21 years old. Sometimes we didn't have one of the grades. We had first through eighth, and when we moved to that area from a different area of West Virginia, I was in third grade. So, I attended there from third grade through sixth grade. We had one teacher, it was her job (pause), and we had one room with a little kitchen. It was her job to make sure that everyone had reading, math, Social Studies, and all the other subjects. So, we learned a lot by listening. If she was talking with some eighth graders about some subject, and you wanted to know about it, you could listen. There was a table up front where she would take each of the classes.

**Albrecht:** So, one simple question: Thinking back over your 70 years, who was your favorite teacher?

**Duckworth:** That would never be hard to figure out... when I was in Parker Hill School, Irene Waltz. I don't know how she did what she did, but she is the one who influenced me. She had a great influence on me. I didn't really think that when I was in third or fourth grade. I was painting a watercolor. There wasn't anything to it, but she decided that she was going to frame it. And, she took it to an exhibit in Morgantown, and it won a ribbon, and I think it was one of the first times that I became interested in art. One afternoon, when I became a teacher, in a teachers' workroom, for some really odd reason, I began talking about Ms. Waltz, and I never really discussed her to others before or said what a great person she was. Through college, I maintained a friendship with her. She lived near the college. So, I would visit her. But, this day I was talking in the teachers' workroom, and on that same day that I was talking about her, Linda (Stephen's wife) placed a newspaper on the table in front of me, and it was her obituary. The day that she died, I spoke about her, and I always feel a closeness in her spirit, and (pause) it has continued in me as a teacher.

**Albrecht:** Three words to describe Ms. Waltz…

**Duckworth:** Efficient. Loving. Caring.

---

### Reflection:

What would happen if every student—every day, in every school—felt successful? What impact would success have on students' resiliency, confidence, and self-concept? How would a feeling of success affect behavior? Stephen felt successful that day when Ms. Waltz framed his watercolor painting and displayed it. Stephen is now seventy. That event, that one single event, happened over sixty years ago and gave him a life-vision as well as self-confidence, a hobby, and a career. The smallest event, comment, or action done by a teacher can have a lifelong impact on a student. Teachers have that power.

Worldwide, three content areas in schools have considerable control over how students see themselves. Those areas are math, reading, and writing. For the most part, if a student does well in these three areas, they feel successful. However, just because a student is strong at something does not mean they are passionate about it. And, if a student struggles in math, reading, or writing, school can be challenging.

There is a growing downward trend of students' abilities to do well in math, reading, and writing. This is concerning. Students need to be proficient in these content areas. What is the root cause? After twenty-five years in education it is obvious that a combination of factors has played a role in this trend. Poverty, repeated taught behaviors from one generation to another, technological distractions, absenteeism, and apathy can all be identified as some of the causes for lowered skill trends. These factors do have negative impacts. They can also be used as excuses, too. However, as I see it, there is one factor that in recent years has trumped all others: standardization. Schools are publicly funded, and as long as they are, the investors are the taxpayers. Taxpayers want equity, but like fingerprints, no town in America is the same. Each town faces its own set of history, challenges, culture, zones of tolerance, and beliefs.

Most educational laws and standards in the United States are governed at the state level. Though this practice of dividing educational power by states sounds like values can be managed more locally than nationally, there is still widespread diversity within every state. Setting standards must be done thoughtfully and carefully, so that the individual interests and needs of every student and community are met. To provide equity through standardization, individual necessities and interests have been undervalued. When these are not met, students will not grow at their greatest potential in the areas that most state and federal standards are focused on. This causes a further domino effect. Lower skill sets have a direct impact on success and self-esteem. Change in education needs to happen to get more students feeling successful at school, and it starts with action. Schools have been hoping for changes; having hope is essential, but without action, hope just remains optimism. Action begins with two mindsets:

1. All students are capable of success.
2. All students are talented in some way.

Once per week, each of my students presents a current event to the class. I give the students many resources, but the topics are entirely left up to them. In November of 2010, a student of mine named Brian reported a current event about a bottle that had been found on a German beach. The bottle contained a message thrown from a cruise ship by a five-year-old boy twenty-five years prior. The letter was returned to that boy, now a 31-year-old man. The story made worldwide news. The event captured the attention of my student, Brian, and the class.

We have open discussions after each presentation. It was CJ who said, "We should do that," but Anthony took it upon himself to go home and tell his mother about it. It just so happened that

Anthony's mother was in the food catering business, and it was a relatively easy task for her to procure the four cases of empty wine bottles that her son requested. In early December, with no forewarning, 48 semi-scrubbed wine bottles showed up in my classroom. The four boxes had a simple note on top stating, "Cool idea." I panicked. Wine bottles in my classroom?!?

When the kids arrived that morning, I saw many of them going up to Anthony, saying, "You did it!" Now I knew where the bottles came from. There was no going back after my class insisted that we send messages in bottles like the boy in the news story. After coming to grips with having actual wine bottles in my classroom, I agreed. The kids never considered that we live 200 miles from the Atlantic Ocean, and after a little research, I learned that if those bottles were going to travel, they needed to be put in the Gulf Stream, another thirty miles out to sea. Fourth graders do not always see limits. I called my mother, who lived on the coast of North Carolina. She convinced a fishing captain to take the bottles out to sea, and after three weeks of research and writing, the bottles were stuffed and corked.

Right before the holiday break, the boxes of bottles traveled across our icy school parking lot to my car, and in January they headed to North Carolina. In March, the kids watched live on the same Smartboard that Brian presented his current event on as the captain's son and daughter tossed the bottles into the Atlantic. I thought that I was done with the project, but the project was not done with our class.

Ninety days later, a woman in Nova Scotia called the school.

She had found Adam's bottle while walking on the beach. Six months later a letter arrived from the Azores informing us that Curtis's bottle was found. Ten months later a bottle washed up in France. It was Tarrell's, and shortly after that, a fourth bottle arrived in Portugal; it turned out to be Brian's. The final bottle was found on a beach in southern England during the 2012 Summer Olympics Games. It was Michael's. The project was reported on by the Associated Press, and the story went viral. Will another bottle wash up? Most bottles that do reach land quickly get buried in sand. They do not actually float for decades. Most likely many of bottles are buried, waiting for a storm to disturb the shoreline just enough to allow their discovery. Only time will tell. However, like a teacher framing a watercolor painting, these small moments will be remembered. Only time will tell if the memory of these moments will be the catalyst of something significant.

The model for giftedness says that when we combine talent, creativity, and work ethic, a student is gifted. The story of those 43 wine bottles combined the expertise of Brian's research, CJ's ideas, Anthony's creativity to gather wine bottles, and an entire class's motivation to work hard follows the giftedness model.

We want our students to feel successful, but the truth is that not all of them do. Actions will have a footprint on education. So, here is a call to action in six steps that were all part of the message in a bottle project:

- **Step 1: Help the students believe in themselves.** I will never argue against the importance of reading, writing, or math, but the fact is that students need time to develop their gifts, and those talents may not directly fall in those three content areas. The message in a bottle project was entirely student-made. They believed in what they were doing.

- **Step 2: Break the rules of conventional thought.** Releasing forty-three wine bottles into the Atlantic Ocean is way outside the box learning. After graduating, my students still talk about it. The world is starving for creative thinkers. Is education about cramming young minds with the knowledge or is it about helping students fall in love with learning, so that they do it for their entire lives?
- **Step 3: Do not be afraid to fail.** Our class spent three weeks working on researching our area of the world. The letters we wrote had meaning. A lot of time was invested in writing with the potential for no return. We need to teach risk-taking if we expect our students to advance. How often is it that measures are put in place so that a student does not fall flat on their face? It is a mistake to do this. Students need to feel failure so they can learn resilience. There is an increasing trend of young talented students moving back home a year out of high school because the world was harder than they expected, and they did not know how to deal with it.
- **Step 4: Do not change your course because of the naysayers.** Whether through jealousy or nitpicking, some people live to criticize those who try new ideas. When the first bottle was found, some environmentalists questioned the project. However, my class learned that for every person that challenged the project, thousands of people were fascinated

by it. Students need to face opposition and learn to listen to it. After students listened, they needed to be taught to stick to what they believed if they felt they were still correct. However, a balance is needed in which students learn to incorporate new knowledge into their beliefs. That doesn't mean they can't face naysayers, just that they are taught to have an open mind. If they still believe in themselves and their original charge, they need to be encouraged to face naysayers.

- **Step 5: Teach work ethic.** Because the message in a bottle project was student-centered, they worked hard. Their motivation accelerated their writing levels. When we find what students are interested and talented in and teach work ethic in those areas, it transfers to working harder in the areas that are challenging. Work ethic is influenced by the interest people have in what they are doing. If the class only had half of the students working hard, this would have pulled down the work ethic of those that were interested in the project.

- **Step 6: When success is achieved, serve others.** Our students presented their findings about the speed of ocean currents and spread the message about the joy of writing after they were successful. Our success motivated other students to write.

Visionaries realize that programs for the gifted should not exclusively be reserved for those students who have strength in reading, writing, and math. Some students struggle in one or two areas, while others struggle in all three. If students are going to make progress, schools must recognize their natural talents to help them believe in themselves. Instead of teachers and parents pushing students to work, students who believe in themselves are more motivated to try on their own. What is most important is that learning does not stop when school does.

Gifted experiences help students discover self-value and joy, and consequently have a snowball effect on motivation. When gifted programs are limited to those students with talent in math, reading, and writing, a school has been created with disproportionate opportunities. Giftedness needs to be recognized in unconventional ways. In chapter 1, I introduced the mindset of the Reggio Emelia schools. These schools capitalize on the strengths and interests of everyone.

Stephen's interview proves that a focus on the gifts of every student lead to a higher probability for that student to be successful. For a moment in time, his teacher, Ms. Waltz, recognized that Stephen worked hard on his artwork. He was interested in the medium that he was using, and most likely needed a nudge to believe in himself. Ms. Waltz framed his artwork. It was a small act that forever shaped his life. It is interesting to note that Stephen does not fit into the pattern noted in the previous interviews; though he is over fifty, he identified his favorite teacher based on an emotional impact that teacher had made. Stephen is an outlier. Of the 600 interviews I conducted, it was rare to hear about a person over the age of fifty identifying with emotions. Nearly all the people in the cohort over fifty linked their best memories to a teacher that had a strong skill set. The reasons behind this pattern can only be left to conjecture and open a whole new area of investigation. Do our values change as we age, or do different generations value different styles of teaching? As seen in the Emelia Reggio schools, the effects of war stimulated what schools needed to do. Surely, if there are outliers like Stephen, multiple factors come into play.

## Chapter 6
## Rubber Meets Responsibility

(1)

The Roxbury Rubber Company of Boston was the first of its kind. In the 1820s and 30s, the business world was experimenting with a newfound resource: rubber. In 2016, the world's consumption of raw Indian rubber was more than twenty-seven million tons with growth estimates over the next eight years of 2.8 percent annually. Consider all the products that are manufactured with rubber. The mousepad that is sitting beside the computer I am typing on, the bottom of my sneakers, and the tires on my car are all rubber. The track on which my daughter competes is composed of chips of rubber. As the Roxbury Rubber Company began to invent applications for rubber, articles and advertisements for rubber goods began to increase throughout the United States. Companies were taking notice, and Roxbury Rubber started sending products all over the world. People were anxious to try products made with this new substance.

In 1831, 31-year-old Charles Goodyear was scarcely making enough money to survive. Through the 1820s, Goodyear had taken the knowledge he had on hardware and was manufacturing marketable farm implements and tools. Up until this point, most tools similar to those that Goodyear was producing were imported from England. With his hold on the domestic market, Goodyear was slowly but surely acquiring wealth. Goodyear began to invest his money in other business ventures, but his investments faltered miserably. Those failures, coupled with severe dyspepsia—a dysfunction of the digestive system—caused a downhill spiral that went just as fast as Goodyear ascended the ladder of success. Goodyear found himself struggling to develop another path for a profitable business. In desperation, he began reading about the invention of rubber and its uses. A self-taught scientist, he started collecting articles on the topic. The creation of rubber and its infinite variety of possibilities intrigued him.

Goodyear knew about the failure of life preservers and incorporated the use of rubber in a new version of a rubberized life preserver. He traveled to New York to present his idea to the Roxbury Rubber Company. His ingenuity left an impression on the people that he met. Goodyear's idea of using rubberized tubes in life preservers attracted the attention of the manager in charge of the New York branch of the Roxbury Rubber Company. He made a startling confession to Goodyear: their company was on the brink of ruin. To the company's surprise, many of the products made with rubber were rotting and crumbling with age. Thousands of dollars of goods were being rendered useless. When most people may have shrugged their shoulders and written rubber off as a fad of the time, Goodyear devoted himself to seeing if he could create a form of rubber that would not decay.

Unfortunately, his financial troubles caught up with him. Upon returning to Philadelphia, he was arrested because a creditor had filed a lawsuit against him. Goodyear was a persuasive man, and he began looking for additional investors. He discovered that the stickiness of rubber could be reduced by adding magnesium oxide, more commonly known as magnesia. He saw a use for this substance on the soles of shoes, and he began applying it to flannel cloth to reinforce the bottoms of footwear. However, even when the gum of the rubber was treated this way, it grew sticky. Goodyear was balancing discovery with financial collapse. His investors found themselves moving further and further into debt, and with limited success coming from Goodyear's research, they cut economic ties. This still did not sway Goodyear from his path. He moved to New York, took a modest attic apartment with his family, and continued to experiment with the help of a local druggist. He began testing with acids and lead, and through extensive experimentation he was able to stabilize rubber until it came in contact with acids.

The stabilization of rubber began to gain him national attention, so much so that President Andrew Jackson wrote to him about his work. It seemed that Goodyear was again on the road to success, while also teetering on the edge of starvation. The chemicals he was using were causing ill effects on his health, and at one point he nearly killed himself in his lab when he applied nitric acid to lead oxide. Still, Goodyear's improvements were enough to gain a patent on his developments with rubber, and he relocated his manufacturing facility and family to Staten Island. Things were looking promising.

Most Americans are well versed in the economic collapse of 1929, which sparked the Great Depression. Less recognized was the drawn-out recession known as the Panic of 1837. During this eight-year financial crisis, falling cotton prices, together with failed loans, made expanding western companies experience a severe drop in wages. Unemployment reached a staggering 25%, which rivals the Great Depression. The recession caused Goodyear's operation to come to a halt, leaving him penniless once again.

Driven by desperation, Goodyear traveled to the Boston branch of the Roxbury Rubber Company. He was well received and was able to set up a business in Springfield, Massachusetts. His brothers, Nelson and Henry, handled the day to day operations of the business as Charles continued to experiment with rubber. Backed by his wealthy brother-in-law, Goodyear finally perfected the process of vulcanization to stabilize rubber using sulfur. Though it is debatable whether Goodyear was the first in the world to improve the process, he had brought stabilized rubber to the United States market. The creation of stabilized rubber revolutionized thousands of products. Before rubber gaskets, the only way to seal a small gap between moving machine parts was to use leather soaked in oil. Oiled leather can only withstand specific pressures before it leaks. Vulcanized rubber solved this problem. It was easy to mold rubber to exact size specifications. After being put under stress and contorted, rubber recovered quickly and went back to its original dimensions when the pressure was removed. Vulcanized rubber's ability to work as a superior sealant and its durability had a positive effect on the industry.

Though the invention of vulcanized rubber would bring Goodyear some success, he died in 1860. Goodyear had tenacity, and it was his earnest desire to produce high quality products using rubber that would last. The corporate giant, Goodyear Tire and Rubber Company, would not have a connection with its namesake other than the fact that the founder, Frank Seiberling, credited Goodyear for the creation of the substance that would lead to the mass production of tires. It would be Seiberling that would provide Henry Ford with the tubes used on the first automobiles in the early 1900s.

Visionaries see beyond the glaring blocks in the road. Often, a visionary like Charles Goodyear may not see a finished product, but they know when they have encountered a breakthrough. Ms. Waltz, the teacher described in Stephen Duckworth's interview, had a lot in common with Charles Goodyear. She was a visionary too. She saw the hidden talent in young Stephen. She helped him see it for himself. Goodyear saw the potential for vulcanized rubber and put it on display for the world. Many years after the passing of Charles Goodyear, the invention of vulcanized rubber would be tested in the Italian Alps under a completely different set of circumstances.

(2)

IN 1935, VITALE BRAMANI of Turin, Italy lost six close friends in the Italian Alps to a mountaineering disaster. An avid climber, well known guide, and member of the Italian Alpine Club, Bramani led an expedition into the Italian Alps. As the group climbed Mount Rasica, they were entangled in the rage of a snowstorm and dense fog. The conditions worsened to the point that the team could not hike out of the mountains. Tragically, six of Bramani's fellow climbers died from frostbite and exposure. The cause of the accident was attributed to inadequate footwear, which prevented the climbers from descending to safety. Before and during the 1930s, mountaineering shoes were fitted with leather soles and hobnails or steel cleats. This sole was rigid and utilized penetration for gripping power. The boots were poorly insulated. Because they were constructed from leather, when they froze, they became dangerous and slippery. This could delay or even prevent a safe and swift descent out of the mountains. This was the most pronounced obstacle as to why many notable peaks in the world had not been conquered. When Bramani lost his six friends, he had a choice. He could remain devastated, or he could do something about the soles of his boots.

The deaths of the six members of Bramani's crew happened nearly eighty years after Goodyear had mastered the science of vulcanized rubber. By the 1930s, automobiles, motorbikes, and bicycles all had tires made with vulcanized rubber. Together with Leopoldo Pirelli, another Italian, Bramani developed a new lens for looking at the way mountaineering shoes were utilized. Pirelli was creating tires for the fastest cars on the planet. With the financial support of Pirelli, Bramani took two years to create a boot sole that gripped snow and rock, just like Pirelli tires. Vulcanized rubber allowed for a tread to be molded into the rubber sole. The breakthrough saved lives. The soles were called Vibram, a combination of the first and last name of Vitale Bramani. The development of the soles had an immediate effect on the achievements of mountaineers. Bramani created a unique sole mold, which was copied from the treads of military vehicle tires. The patterned design of the soles combined with vulcanized rubber compounds gave mountaineering boots excellent traction that did not freeze or become rigid.

At 28,251 feet above sea level, Mount Godwin-Austen, also named Chhogori, is the second highest mountain in the world. The summit is referred to as K2 because of its location within a numbered series of "K" mountains along the China-Pakistan border. Though it is second in elevation to Mount Everest, it is considered the most challenging mountain in the world to ascend. Mount Everest is not symmetrical, which offers many different climbing routes. However, every route to the summit of K2 is highly technical. As of 2018, only 302 people had successfully reached K2, with a fatality rate of one in every five climbers who attempted to reach the summit. However, there is some data that sheds light on how the invention of rubberized mountaineering soles has improved the odds of conquering K2.

The development of soles has allowed for a greater gripping crampon to be attached to the sole. Traditionally, crampons were metal plates with spikes that were strapped onto a climber's boot for walking on ice. Though a 20% mortality rate sounds awful, without the developments of Vitali Bramani's vulcanized rubber soles, the mountain may have never had a single person summit. In 1954, a climbing team led by Ardito Desio accompanied by three other climbers reached the summit of K2. They were the pioneering team to succeed and the first team to use boots manufactured by Vitali Bramani. Desio's team consisted of Italians Lino Lacedelli and Achille Compagnoni, as well as a Pakistani climber named Colonel Muhammad Ata-Ullah. Beginning in the 1940s, people were able to witness an incredible rise in successful summiting on some of the most challenging climbs thanks to the advancement in footwear.

On May 29th, 1953, Sir Edmund Hillary and Nepalese Sherpa mountaineer Tenzing Norgay became the first confirmed climbers to reach the summit of Mount Everest. It was not the only feat in Hillary's long and famous career as an explorer. He would also be the first explorer to conquer the North and the South Poles. Hillary wore a Vibram sole. Jim Whittaker, the first North American to climb Mount Everest, wore them too. Vibram has become the gold standard for performance rubber soles and compounds. Footwear makers use Vibram on a range of athletic, casual, military, and industrial footwear.

Charles Goodyear developed vulcanized rubber nearly 80 years before it was being used for the soles of boots designed by Vitali Bramani. Both advancements transformed the world in manufacturing and mountaineering, respectively. Though their ideas were revolutionary, the paths that they carved to get to their destinations were starkly different. It could be argued that Goodyear was obsessed with the improvement of long-lasting rubber products, because he had plenty of opportunities to simply drop the whole idea and move on. This was not in his DNA. There are qualities in Goodyear that most inventors share. He had an absolute obsession and tenacity in the face of trial and error over long periods of time. Goodyear would see little profit from the invention of vulcanized rubber, but he would die having the satisfaction that he was the first to perfect vulcanized rubber's chemistry and hold the patent to prove it.

Bramani, on the other hand, was an inventor out of necessity. He was a mountain climber but had suffered the loss of six team members due to inadequate equipment. His experience put him in the mindset to search for a solution. The nature of a person and the nurturing they receive throughout their life has an impact on their reaction to challenges. When inventions fail, it is not necessarily the idea that is weak. The new development was unable to fulfill a need. Vulcanized rubber was an upgrade for so many products worldwide that it became a permanent replacement. If there are mountain climbers, rubber mountaineering soles are essential.

Arguably, Thomas Edison is one of the most successful American inventors of all time. One thousand and ninety-three patents in the United States are linked to his name. This number does not include the many patents held by Edison in France, Germany, and the United Kingdom. His inventions significantly changed the world. He made notable advancements by creating electric light, sound recordings, and motion pictures. Edison's inventions allowed for enormous leaps in the telecommunication industry. His contributions include the stock ticker, a device to record votes, and battery powered automobiles. However, not all of Edison's ideas had lasting effects.

Vulcanized rubber became a widely used product because of its effectiveness. The timing of its development was perfect because a widespread need for it existed in multiple areas. Within the timeline of Edison's inventions, there was an idea that never gained momentum. Edison thought it was foolish to have multiple books all on different subjects. He proposed a unique idea that was significantly ahead of its time. Edison proposed the idea of a thick metal book filled with all the information that someone might need. The book would be made of lightweight and inexpensive nickel. This metal was reasonably priced and readily available. Cheap to buy and lighter than stacks of books, the metal book would be more durable than its paper counterparts. In Edison's mind, the low cost of the book would advance the education of people with less money. The book would not fray or deteriorate with age, and people would not have to worry about pages being ripped. The reader could even read in the rain. When discussing this idea, Edison stated, "Why not? Such a book would weigh only a pound. I can make a pound of nickel sheets for a dollar and a quarter."

Why did the metal book idea fail to flourish? At the time, it had neither a way to be updated nor an interested audience. Those ideas which become widespread, highly manufactured, and redeveloped have sustaining power. Goodyear's vulcanized rubber had vast potential in the industry, and it could be adapted to solve safety issues in mountaineering. The timing of the invention of vulcanized rubber was perfect. It was developed at the cusp of an industrial revolution, and advancements in transportation were coming. The automobile was just decades away from the marketplace. When Edison proposed a one stop shop book, it did not catch on. Its timing was poor. Edison was born in 1847. Had Thomas Edison been born in 1947, he would have been in his 40s during the infancy of the internet. The internet revolutionized the way we get information. It is a lot like a single book, a one stop shop for all useful information. Edison's idea was solid, but his timing and technology were off by about a century. Had Thomas Edison been born just 100 years later, would we be talking about him in the same breath as Bill Gates and Steve Jobs? Quite possibly.

(3)

IN 1933, THE CINCINNATI-BASED soap company, Kutol, was on the verge of bankruptcy. Founded in 1912, Kutol was a manufacturer of domestic and industrial cleaning products. The business had struggled for years to be profitable. A stroke of luck would save this modest company.

Before the late 1940s, most houses were heated with coal. Coal was used because it was less expensive than wood and more energy efficient. The use of coal for heating produced a fine sooty layer of dust. Because of this, cleaning products were formulated to remove coal soot residue. Wallpaper was stylish in the 1920s and 30s. Many homes had flaws on the bare walls. Paint would not cover those imperfections, so wallpaper was a simple way to make a not-so-perfect wall look good at an inexpensive price. Wallpaper had its challenges too. The wallpaper of the 1930s was entirely different from the vinyl wallpaper of today. Vinyl wallpaper can be cleaned with a soap and water mixture, but coal soot was not as easily removed from the wallpaper from the early part of the 20th century.

In 1883, Bernard Kroger founded the Kroger Company, which ultimately became the Kroger grocery chain. In 2018, Kroger ranked number one as the largest grocery chain in the United States. In the 1930s, its most robust market remained in and around Cincinnati. Kroger needed a local low-cost company to create soap for cleaning coal soot off of wallpaper. Since Kutol was local, representatives from Kroger worked with Cleo McVicker, the family owner of Kutol, to become their sole manufacturer of a soot cleaning product. Desperate to keep Kutol afloat, McVicker agreed to manufacture 15,000 cases of soot cleaner. Little did Kroger know that McVicker had no idea how to make this cleaning product. With some hard work, McVicker and his brother, Noah, researched the formulation, filled the order, and saved the company. This deal kept Kutol profitable for nearly a decade.

After World War II, homes in the United States began to be heated with oil and gas furnaces. With the change from coal to oil heating, the cleaning product market shifted. Essentially, soot cleaning products were no longer needed. Once again, Kutol faced bankruptcy. To compound Kutol's problems, Cleo McVicker was killed in 1949 in an airplane accident, leaving his twenty-five-year-old nephew, Joe McVicker, in charge of a company whose main product becoming obsolete. The company barely continued to get by under Joe McVicker's leadership.

Luck can play a role in success. A person can walk into a gas station, buy a scratch off ticket, and suddenly be rich. Kutol was a company that needed to roll the dice, and they were about to. In 1954, Joe McVicker's niece, Kay Zufall, was teaching nursery school. She needed a product for the children to make Christmas ornaments. Zufall read in a craft magazine about a way of using wallpaper cleaner to make Christmas ornaments. Knowing that her uncle was barely making ends meet, she bought Kutol's wallpaper cleaner for the project. This choice would be the spark that would ignite fiscal growth. Zufall noticed that her students loved playing with the doughy mixture, and she relayed this back to McVicker. After some brainstorming, the detergent was removed from the wallpaper cleaner, coloring was added, and a subtly scented almond paste was mixed in to give the dough a unique and pleasant smell. The new product was much more kid friendly. The mixture was repackaged as a new toy for children and renamed Kutol's Rainbow Modeling Compound. Zufall believed this was not a great marketing name for a children's product and convinced her uncle to rebrand it as Play-Doh.

Play-Doh was not an instant success. Growth was slow, and it was sold almost exclusively to schools, with very little making it to the retail market. As a wallpaper cleaner, a can of cleaning formula sold for $0.34; the same amount of Play-Doh was selling for $1.50. The interest in the dough drove the price up. Play-Doh was a unique entertainment product for young and creative minds. Although Play-Doh had growth, it was not expanding at the rate Joe McVicker was hoping. McVicker understood there was another critical element of success that would play a vital role in Play-Doh becoming a household brand.

Robert James Keeshan was born on June 27th, 1927. Like many men of that era, he enlisted in World War II. Robert entered military life in 1945 as a Marine, and he was assigned to be part of the Pacific war campaign while he was still stationed in the United States. By the time Play-Doh had been fully developed, Keeshan, now a retired Marine, was finding his way into the hearts of many American children through his popular television series, Captain Kangaroo. After much effort, McVicker was able to get an audience with Keeshan. McVicker showed him Play-Doh. McVicker realized that his company's main obstacle was a lack of funding for a regional or national advertising campaign, but he observed the rapid advancements in television programming aimed at children. If Play-Doh was to make it into the hearts of youth across the country, television would be the perfect path for that to happen. Keeshan loved the product, and soon a deal was struck. Captain Kangaroo would use the product on the show once a week for a 2% stake in Kutol. Kutol had now overcome its main obstacle: lack of publicity.

At the end of 1958, after being on the market for only one year, Play-Doh's sales reached over three million dollars. In 1998, Play-Doh was inducted into the National Toy Hall of Fame, and in 2003, the Toy Industry Association named Play-Doh as one of the 100 most memorable and creative toys of the twentieth century. Today, Play-Doh's production is close to 100 million tubs of dough per year.

Play-Doh allows for creativity, fills an entertainment need for children, and has endurance and longevity. At its inception, Play-Doh had the same impact and characteristics for the toy industry that vulcanized rubber had made in manufacturing. However, the sales of Play-Doh did not catch fire on their own. The factors of luck and publicity were critical in creating success. Many great products will never reach their full potential because inventors often do not have the means or the know-how to present their idea to the world. In the case of Play-Doh, Captain Kangaroo bestowed both the means and the know-how.

(4)

IN 1888, EDWARD BELLAMY of Massachusetts published the book *Looking Backward*. It was the third bestselling novel of that time, only outsold by Harriet Beecher Stowe's *Uncle Tom's Cabin* and Lew Wallace's *Ben-Hur: The Tale of Christ*. The novel's setting took place in the 1870s and 1880s. This era was defined by several peaks and valleys in the world economy. Many labor unions were exercising strikes to control big business, and with emotions running high, demonstrations sometimes became hostile and dangerous. On May 4th, 1886, at Haymarket Square in Chicago, a peaceful rally commenced. Workers were protesting to limit the maximum number of hours an employer could assign per day. The rally was partially a reaction to the killing of several workers the day before by police.

At some point during the May 4th demonstration, an unknown person threw an explosive device at police as they acted to disperse the public protest. Gunfire erupted. In the end, seven police officers and at least four civilians were killed. Many people were wounded. Bellamy was an author who saw the chaos erupting in the workplace. He believed greater harmony and peace should exist with an increase in consistency between the operation of factories and the regulations that governed them. Though his book would be considered a socialist approach to the industry, Bellamy never claimed to support socialism and, in fact, supported the practice of free market trade. Many other authors were penning books similar to Bellamy. Unlike other authors, however, Bellamy had developed a system in his book that was entirely new: credit cards. Never before had the concept of a credit card been described.

The success of a product depends on the alignment of many factors. There needs to be a pioneering concept, a large-scale need, and the product or idea needs exposure. Timing is also important. For example, when Edison had proposed a comprehensive metal book of all knowledge, his timing was off, and the product failed. However, the introduction of the concept of a credit card could not have come at a better time. Bellamy's credit card did not operate like modern credit cards. What Bellamy suggested was much like a citizen's dividend.

In the 5th century in Athens, Greece, a large vein of silver was discovered. It was recommended that each of the citizens of Athens each get an equal share. They were given government credit for a corresponding portion of the silver found. Edward Bellamy considered this a form of credit that could be used by citizens.

In 1927, inspired by Bellamy, the Farrington Manufacturing Company developed the Charga-Plate. This metal card, like a military dog tag, had raised numbers that were embossed onto a charge slip. This system saved the time of handwriting out a bill of sale.

In smaller towns, a person's Charga-Plate was held at a place of business, but in larger cities, the owner of the card would hold and present it much like a modern credit card. There was no banking system for the money or transactions to filter though. Therefore, the Charga-Plate was not universally embraced. Some merchants did not want to accept this system out of the fear of not collecting a debt; hence the success of the Charga-Plate was inconsistent. One of the largest sectors of credit card use was at the gas pump. Gas stations were seeing enormous growth in sales as the number of automobile owners grew. When using the Charga-Plate, the customer was getting a short-term loan, and transactions were made with higher speed.

In 1958, Bank of America would become the first financial institution to take a stab at the opportunities that credit cards held. In September of that year, BankAmericard was launched in Fresno, California. At the time, 45% of the residents of Fresno had accounts at Bank of America. This made it an ideal location to launch a credit card system tied to a bank. The 45% consumer base gave credit cards widespread exposure. Much like Play-Doh, Bank of America needed to get their brand on display to a broad audience. Fresno was the perfect city. By sending out sixty thousand credit cards to all of their customers that month, the bank essentially forced merchants to accept the use of a credit card. Over time, Bank of America licensed the use of their credit card product to other banks, and universally the credit card became known as Visa.

For a product to reach global success, three key elements must be in place. First, the product must fill a universal need. Like vulcanized rubber, credit cards did this by making purchases more manageable for both customers and businesses. Second, the product must have a captive audience that wants it. Play-Doh's audience was young children. Vulcanized rubber revolutionized a vast variety of industries, and credit cards were desirable because they made purchases faster and easier. Lastly, a product must have a strong consumer base. Credit cards do. Early on, banks issued them to people whom they saw as risks for debt. Banks would charge a small interest rate for overdue payments, like a loan. Many people made late payments, and the banks raked in enormous profits.

As the market for credit became more competitive, banks became riskier. Credit cards were issued to nearly everyone. The product was successful, but the impact on the health of society was not ethical. The early distribution of credit cards was imperfect. Cards were given to people who had difficulty maintaining jobs, drug addicts, and compulsive spenders. No application was filled out. The bank simply sent cards to everyone. In 1968, Lyndon Johnson's Special Assistant for Consumer Affairs, Betty Furness, reported that the distribution of credit cards was "like giving candy to a baby." By 1970, the practice of sending a card was made illegal. An application process was put in place. But at this point, people were so accustomed to the system of using credit cards that reversing it would be like telling a mountain climber to strip the rubber from his mountaineering boots. It just was not going to happen.

In the case of mountaineering, the change of leather and nail boot soles to vulcanized rubber soles saved lives. What can be said about the addiction to credit cards? Many studies show that when paying with a credit card, people are likely to spend more. It makes perfect sense. If a consumer goes into a hardware store to buy a lawnmower, it would be highly unlikely for that person to whip out hundred-dollar bills at the cash register. When using a credit card, there is a disconnect between the actual price and what that means in terms of dollars and cents.

On July 7th, 2011, *Time Magazine* published a story called "Finally, Money Advice That Will Make You Skinnier." The article used research from the *Journal of Consumer Research*. Researchers Manoj Thomas, Kalpesh Kaushik Desai, and Satheeshkuma Seenivasan found that consumers who pay with a credit card are more likely to buy junk food impulsively. People spending cash used better judgment practicing moderation, and selected healthier food. Credit cards increased the consumption of unhealthy food, but money made a person stop for a moment. The method in which payments are made causes consumers to make more thoughtful decisions.

According to the United States Federal Reserve, as of March 2018, Americans alone have a combined personal credit card debt of 1.03 trillion dollars. To make this into a comprehendible number, a December 2017 report by the Federal Reserve explained that if a person takes the total debt on credit cards in the United States alone and divides it by the number of credit cards currently issued, the average debt per United States adult with a credit card is $5,839. According to The National Foundation for Credit Counseling's annual financial literacy surveys, more than one third of all households in the United States follow a system called "revolving debt" on their credit cards. Simply put, the credit card owner keeps paying off the interest on the card while accumulating further debt.

Successful products do not always equate to healthy lifestyles. Products can be unhealthily successful. The creation of the credit card was highly prosperous in terms of its universal use and popularity among people. Like the credit card, though, some products are so successful that consumers have a blindness to the degree that they are abusing the product. The consumer cannot recognize that the success of the product could potentially lead to their misfortune. This is dangerous territory to enter.

(5)

ON SEPTEMBER 13TH, 2012, the New York City Board of Health voted unanimously to ratify the Sugary Drinks Portion Cap Rule (known as the Soda Ban). The regulation stated that there would be a 16-ounce limit on soft drinks served in New York City. The law was based on reports that confirmed the unhealthy effects of sugar. It had been long understood that increased levels of sugar led to weight gain, and the City of New York was working to do something about this crisis. Supported heavily by Mayor Michael Bloomberg, the rule took effect on March 12th, 2013. The real issue was not sugary soft drinks. The problem was the increasing fight against obesity. According to the *Journal of Health Economics*, in the period following 2010, the United States spent over 190 million dollars on obesity-related health issues. Was the Soda Ban about preserving our health, our economy, or both?

Soft drinks trace their roots back to Leeds, England. In 1767, Joseph Priestly invented carbonated water. He created it by infusing water with carbon dioxide and hanging a vat of it over fermenting beer. In 1771, chemistry professor Torbern Bergman was suffering from poor health. He reproduced naturally effervescent mineral spring waters, which were thought by many civilizations at the time to cure diseases. The carbonation in this medical drink was believed to help the sick, so pharmacists primarily created its formula. In 1835, the first bottled soda water was produced in the United States. As the local drugstores evolved into the central attraction in most American towns and neighborhoods, the pharmacist was in charge of the manufacturing and distribution of soda. Incredibly, up until 1914, some soda was mixed with caffeine and cocaine as an over the counter prescription.

Root beer was first introduced in 1878, and the flavor called cola was created in 1881. Since then, the flavor variations have been endless. However, one key ingredient has been consistent in nearly all varieties of soda: sugar. According to the Coca-Cola Company, standard soft drink sizes have increased through the decades. When first bottled in the 1940s, bottles held 6.5 ounces. The twelve-ounce can was introduced in the 50s and became the market standard in the 1960s. In the early 1990s, sixteen- and twenty-ounce bottles were introduced. The trend shows that people are consuming more soda and in larger sizes. A 2006 study published in the journal *Pediatrics* found that replacing sugary beverages with water led to a significant drop in weight in adolescents.

Was the Soda Ban justified? Should sugary drinks be portioned at a reasonable level so that people can lead healthier lives?

According to the highest court in New York State, the Court of Appeals, the answer was clear. On March 24th, 2014, the court unanimously overturned the Soda Ban. New Yorkers could go back to drinking any size soda they wanted to. There are parallels at the national level. On January 16th, 1919, the 18th amendment to the United States Constitution was passed, which prohibited the sale of alcohol and began the Prohibition Era. Fourteen years later, the United States reversed the amendment with the 21st amendment, ending prohibition.

In 1970, laws were passed that did not allow credit card companies to drop-send an activated credit card because there was widespread abuse. Instead, an application had to be mailed that would go through a review process to assess consumer responsibility. This regulation has never been overturned. In the cases of soda and credit cards, both products were and still are highly successful. They fulfill strong consumer desires, are innovative, and capture a broad audience. However, in both cases, there has been an adverse effect on the consumer when the purchaser cannot scale back the usage of the product on their own. Statistically, one out of every three people reading this book has rollover credit card debt. This means that the consumer is getting by with merely paying the interest on their debt. Like sugary drinks, our freedoms allow us to make poor personal long-term decisions. Who is ultimately responsible for each person? Do the large companies behind the products have a responsibility beyond a simple warning label to help consumers make the right decisions?

Michelle Obama made healthy eating and childhood obesity

a top platform priority while she was the First Lady of the United States. In 2009, she cited a study prepared by the Centers for Disease Control and Prevention and RTI International. In 2006, these groups had found that the direct and indirect cost of all issues related to obesity in the United States alone cost close to $147 billion annually. Though this study has some age, people's habits have not changed. Obesity issues in the United States continue to rise. Going back to a study done some years ago is valuable and relevant because it illustrates a trend. The study pointed out that people deemed as obese spent an average of $1,429 more for their medical care per year than did people that were not in the obese range on the Body Mass Index or BMI. The trend in the United States is not improving. Statistics released by the Center for Disease Control for the year 2015 found that 39.8% of Americans, amounting for a population of 93.3 million people, are clinically obese. There are not only health risks due to obesity, but the effects on the rise in healthcare costs are substantial.

The statistics omit a serious part of the obesity debate. Obesity is caused by several factors, often in combination. There is a cost factor. Unhealthy food generally costs less. The decisions of the local supermarket to run sales on certain food can affect the health of a community. Time is another factor that has caused an increase in weight gain. The time preparation required for home cooking healthy food and finding the time to exercise regularly in an increasingly work-centric world is challenging.

Vulcanized rubber, the rubber soles on shoes, Play-Doh, credit cards, and soft drinks have all been historically successful products. Each commodity is widely used or consumed in the United States and throughout the world. Beyond success, what are the moral obligations of a manufacturer versus the personal responsibilities of the consumer? During Prohibition and the Soda Ban, the state and federal governments felt that the answer was quite clear. The products were banned. These are black and white decisions, and if the public complied, the effects and results would become even more black and white. However, in both cases, many people felt that these rulings stifled people's freedom to choose for themselves. This pushed the issue into the gray area, and these two products are only part of a vast market of consumables that have had the same effect.

The challenges of working through the complex and adverse effects of successful products is not a simple one-step fix, and compromise can be difficult to reach. There is a line that, when crossed, leads to greed. Greed is when the adverse effect of a successful product is ignored at the expense of the consumer. If this is the case, companies and governments do have a moral responsibility to guide consumers. Guide is the key word here; guidance, not protection, is what is needed. Each person is responsible for making their own decisions. If one person makes a poor decision, it is not someone else's responsibility to take care of the consequences. People need to own up to the implications of the decisions they make, whether those decisions are intentional or not. Quick fixes are embraced because they take care of a problem promptly. Nobody wants lingering issues. However, consumer responsibility and production ethics are not quick fixes. They require education, time, and patience. Also, not every person who gets an education will fully embrace or even understand what they are learning. Temptations sometimes outweigh well thought out decisions. There is a growing need for people to talk about how to live healthier lives through decision making. These conversations start in our homes and schools, followed by our communities. Community values need to be reflected in our schools. A definite line between what is right and wrong is difficult to distinguish because each home has its own set of values. If a school advocates and teaches a different set of moral principles, whether correct or incorrect, students suffer because they get conflicting messages.

Getting homes, schools, and communities to have a universally similar reaction to challenges requires frequent, predictable, and proactive conversations. When people come together to discuss problems before they surface, better education can be provided. There needs to be wider solutions that are necessary for people to make better decisions. Even if a person knows that he or she is making a negative decision, they may still make it even if the proper support systems are in place. If a family must choose between eating McDonald's every night or making one or two healthy meals due to financial concerns, the family is going to eat at McDonald's. They may know that this is not a healthy choice, but realistically it is the only one available. The availability of time and money are two of the largest challenges facing most family's decisions.

The United States Constitution guarantees that citizens are not subservient to the government. The government works for the people. It is the government's job to hold companies that cross the line of greed accountable. The government is designed to protect its citizens, while balancing this with the freedom to make individual choices. It is difficult to make sure that people are well-informed and have the opportunity to work with one another to unconventionally form good habits.

Having insight into how current choices affect each of us in the long term is not easy. I wish you the best of luck in making your own informed decisions.

# Interview with Jahana Hayes
February 2, 2018
Palo Alto, California

*I first met Jahana Hayes in California as part of the induction training for state teachers of the year. Hayes is from Connecticut, was a history teacher, and is a National Teacher of the Year. She would be awarded the glass apple by Barack Obama during his last year in the White House. Hayes was 45 years old when I interviewed her. A few months after this interview, Hayes decided to enter politics and was elected to the United States Congress representing the 5th Congressional District of Connecticut. Hayes was quoted in a 2016 article of the Washington Post as believing, "We've spent a lot of time in the last few years talking about the things that are not working. We really need to shift our attention to all the things that are working."*

**Albrecht:** Well, today is Groundhog's Day, and I am here with…
**Hayes:** Jahana Hayes.
**Albrecht:** You are from?
**Hayes:** Connecticut.
**Albrecht:** Where do you teach?
**Hayes:** Kennedy High School. I am a high school history teacher, but I have not been there in two years though, well, a year and a half. (Note: The National Teacher of the Year is required to take time off from work to lead professional development and advocate

for positive growth in education.)

**Albrecht:** And, you are the National Teacher of the Year.

**Hayes:** Yes, the National Teacher of the Year.

**Albrecht:** OK, just one simple question for you. Who was your favorite teacher of all time?

**Hayes:** I've been asked that question. That is not a simple question because I have been asked that question so many different times this year on my journey. There is not just one person. I was a kid who truly relied on my village. I had a broken family, and I had so many teachers, and it's interesting. When I was named National Teacher of the Year, I talked about a teacher who was not a good teacher and said some really painful things to me. It was crazy that after all of the celebration, and I was at the height of my career, I still remember that teacher. It just taught me that our jobs are so powerful and long lasting, but I think I was always one of those people that thought [pause], I always knew that I wanted to be a teacher. I was born to be a teacher. I played with dolls, lined them up. So, I could name so many [pause]. I could name a guidance counselor, at the point when I was in the high school, and I kind of dropped out, and she would come to my house. She kept coming to my house, bringing me pamphlets and information about alternative programs and even before her, I still don't have an answer for that question yet. Sorry.

**Albrecht:** What high school?

**Hayes:** In my same town, it's called Crosby High School. It's right across town. It is the rival high school for where I teach.

## Reflection:

When I first did this interview, I was disappointed. Most of the time, the question of who your favorite teacher is one that catches people off guard. Out of the hundreds of interviews that I have done, this interview is unique because Hayes had thought about this question many times before. As a National Teacher of the Year, she had been repeatedly asked about her favorite teacher. After I did this interview, I believed it was an outlier and did not fully represent what I was trying to find out. I was searching for the answer that contained a person's raw gut instinct. This interview was nothing like that. It was not drawn out with many pauses for thought. I purposefully put the word 'pause' in Hayes' interview to show how little she paused. Each pause was around two seconds. The fact that she acknowledged that this is not a simple question shows that she fully understands the question. Defining who is a favorite teacher is extremely complex.

A reflection about who a favorite teacher is often tells more information about the person I am interviewing than the educator that they are remembering. A student-teacher interaction is much like a puzzle being put together. If two puzzle pieces are analogous to a teacher and a student, there is as much revealed about the student as there is about the favorite teacher when a person reflects about a beloved teacher. As time goes on, the mind writes its own narrative about how it wants to remember history.

Jahana Hayes proves that all people are capable of success.

She admitted that she was close to dropping out of school. Hayes came from a broken family. She nearly did not make it out of high school. Twenty-five years later she was introduced by President Obama as the National Teacher of the Year. Three years after that, she was elected to the United States Congress. It is an amazing story, and one that may be lost. If a statue was to be built of Jahana Hayes, what would the inscription on the wall behind the statue read? Such a statue does not exist, but certainly the inscription would memorialize Hayes as the National Teacher of the Year and as a United States Congresswoman. Would the inscription also include something about overcoming adversity?

The way a person is remembered in history is as much about the people writing the history as the person that the history is about. With electronic media platforms such as Twitter, Facebook, and Instagram being a regular part of many people's days, we live in a look at me world. This type of world naturally gravitates toward acknowledging achievements and bottom lines. Awards, wins, high grades, faster speeds, and many other measurable outcomes are highly valued. The process and work that it takes to reach a mark of distinction lives in the shadow of the achievement. If Hayes' history was memorialized today, there would be no mention of her resilience and work ethic because history writers want to note achievements, not the process or obstacles that were overcome to get there. Navigating the messy process to overcome obstacles is the greatest achievement of Hayes' life.

Hayes' interview is a reminder to be kind. Teachers bear a tremendous responsibility. Students, even in college, remember a lot about their experiences with teachers. Very small actions have huge effects on students.

Billy was my student for two years. There was a time in my career that I kept the same class for 4th and 5th grade. Early on in teaching, I learned that few things frustrate a teacher more than glitter. I do like sparkle on projects, but the problem with glitter is that it does not stay on the projects. Once it gets into a carpet, it still will be found after a vacuum goes over the floor a dozen times, and I will be stuck wearing it home. Glitter gets in hair and clothing, and it sticks around for years. Billy made a project in 5th grade full of red glitter. Fifteen years later, I ran into Billy. He was working the paint counter at a Lowe's Home Improvement Store. He instantly reverted back to me not being at all happy with the mess of glitter he coated our classroom with when it disintegrated off of a book project he made for school. I had forgotten the whole incident, but it was the first thing Billy talked about. It still seemed to bother him. No teacher is perfect.

Though she does not go into detail, Hayes' incident with a teacher seems like a much rougher set of circumstances. No matter how small, Jahana Hayes' recollection of an awful teacher entered her mind when asked to recall a favorite teacher. Hayes was forty-five years old when I interviewed her. High school was nearly thirty years behind her. Words are powerful, and depending on who those words come from, they can have a lifelong effect.

# Chapter 7
## The Curious Circumstances of the Jefferson Memorial and Paul Revere

(1)

ABRAHAM LINCOLN, THE 16th President of the United States and one of the most prolific examples of American heritage, grew up as a poor young man on an expanding frontier. He read books by candlelight. Hours of reading in his youth would serve Lincoln well in many capacities later in life. Growing up, Lincoln served as a store clerk, a river trader, and a rail splitter; he was highly literate, but he never shied away from hard physical labor. He spoke in plain words that ordinary people could understand. As a lawyer, he merged his profession with his passion for the written word. Guided by his principles, he eventually made a career change and entered politics. He served in the Illinois State Legislature and then the United States Congress, and finally became the President of the United States. Lincoln was assassinated on April 14th, 1865, just as the Civil War was ending. The story of Lincoln is well known by historians who have tried to capture his life. However, whether intentional or unintentional, historians are human with biases and sometimes even hidden agendas.

One of the most iconic monuments in America was erected to honor the legacy of Abraham Lincoln. Nearly eight million people visit the Lincoln Memorial in Washington, D.C. annually; it is a destination for bus tours, school trips, and visitors from all around the world. This monument came to be through early proposals in March of 1867 when Congress created the Lincoln Monument Association. Their charge was to build a memorial dedicated to the memory of Lincoln's ideals. This commission was established less than two years after Lincoln's death. With the dust not nearly close to settling in the aftermath of the American Civil War, the commission decided that this monument was going to be a place of reflection, quiet, and peace. Almost a century later, Dr. Martin Luther King would speak to over 500,000 people from the steps of the Lincoln Memorial in protest about the inequalities between people in the United States. Many other marches and protests have been held at the Lincoln Memorial. Ironically, a place that was designated for quiet reflection has been the location for many rallies. Sometimes, the original purpose of an endeavor takes unexpected turns. Predicting the future is nearly as easy as flipping a pancake blindfolded.

The initial construction of the Lincoln Memorial (on February 12th, 1914) began 105 years after Lincoln was born. Due to the challenges of planning and constructing a monument, the actual construction began just shy of forty-seven years after the original commission was put together. Members of the commission could not agree on where they should build, who should be the architect, and how the monument should look. At one point, a second architect worked his way into the discussion, creating a two-horse race of who was going to build this structure. There was quite a lot of arguing and lobbying happening, and a whole lot of nothing was getting done.

Another challenge was real estate. There was not a lot of it. At the time, the Potomac River passed just west of the Washington Monument. When Lincoln was in the White House, the location where the Lincoln Memorial now sits was the middle of the Potomac River. In 1885, once the Army Corps of Engineers finished the building of the Washington Monument, more land was needed for more monuments. They were commissioned to push the Potomac River three quarters of a mile to the west to create this considerable extension for the nation's new front yard. The project was not completed until 1905, a rather short amount of time given the challenges that they faced.

In 1909, as the nation was celebrating the 100th anniversary of the birth of Abraham Lincoln, the discussion about the future Lincoln Memorial was amplified. The anniversary coincided with the gift of the 3020 Yoshino cherry trees that were given to the United States from Japan to be planted around the Tidal Basin and along the new Potomac shoreline to make the new land look like a settled park.

(2)

MARION ANDERSON WAS a world renowned African American opera singer. She often performed at the White House for Franklin and Eleanor Roosevelt, who were devoted fans of her work. Anderson performed and lived in Washington, D.C. Her shows were growing in such popularity that the sponsors of her concerts, Howard University and the newly formed NAACP, were always facing the challenge of finding her a larger auditorium. Many of the large stages across the United States were not being shared with minorities.

In the early spring of 1939, the sponsors of Anderson's concerts approached the Daughters of the American Revolution to inquire about renting out their new state-of-the-art auditorium, Constitution Hall. Even today, Constitution Hall is considered a hotspot for performers because of its superb acoustics. In 1939, the Daughters of the American Revolution had a stringent racial policy: no black entertainers allowed.

The decision put First Lady Eleanor Roosevelt in a real predicament. She could not disagree more with the denial of the request for the concert hall. Roosevelt was very proud of her association with the Daughters of the Revolution, but she was also known as a strong supporter of social justice and the Civil Rights Movement. It is because of Roosevelt that many African Americans defected from the Republican party of Lincoln to that of the Democratic party of Franklin D. Roosevelt. They made this shift because they finally felt that with Eleanor Roosevelt, a true friend in the White House, they had a voice in politics. Roosevelt realized that the leadership of the Daughters of the Revolution was not willing to show any flexibility concerning a reversal of their stance on African Americans. Seeking to show her support for Anderson, she submitted her resignation as a member.

Roosevelt then went to the public. She wrote a newspaper column to explain to the nation why she had taken this step. She adamantly disagreed with the racial policies of the Daughters of the American Revolution. Years later, many historians give Roosevelt credit for the reforms that were about to occur concerning race in Washington. As time stretches further away from a historical event, credit is often misplaced. In this case, a widely publicized event would change the course of the way people see the Lincoln Memorial and the meaning behind it.

Harold Ickes was the progressive Secretary of the Interior under Franklin Roosevelt. He would stalk the halls at the Department of the Interior, making sure that every resource was used in its entirety. If a person dared to throw away a number two pencil before it was entirely used up, he would make a point to address it. From the first day that Ickes took over the Department of the Interior, he ran the agency as a desegregated institution. Ickes was a white attorney from Chicago, but before joining FDR in Washington, he had served as the president of the Chicago Chapter of the NAACP.

When Howard University and the NAACP could not sway the Daughters of the Revolution to allow Marion Anderson to perform at Constitution Hall, they turned to Harold Ickes for help. They inquired about holding a concert outdoors on the steps of the Lincoln Memorial, sensing that Ickes would be receptive to the idea. Up until this point, the aura surrounding the Lincoln Memorial was much like that of a church: quiet and reflective. It was a place of contemplation. This concert was not consistent with the tone traditionally surrounding the memorial.

Ickes was open to the idea. However, he understood that this was going to get a lot of attention, and so he went straight to President Roosevelt. FDR's response was, "If Marion Anderson wants to sing from the top of the Washington Monument, she has my blessing." With the full backing of the president, this protest concert took place peacefully on the steps of the Lincoln Memorial. Black and white people outfitted in their Sunday best gathered to listen to Anderson's concert, which was also being broadcast nationally. The Roosevelt administration aspired to project a viewpoint of racial harmony. The Roosevelts intentionally did not attend the concert on the steps of the Lincoln Memorial. Had the Roosevelts attended, they would have been the focus of the media. They wanted all of the attention to be given to Marion Anderson. Anderson would return to the same steps as a performer in a memorial concert to sing in the early 1950s after Ickes died. She would revisit one last time in late August of 1963 for the People's March on Washington, when Dr. Martin Luther King Jr. gave his "I Have a Dream" speech.

(3)

THE LINCOLN MEMORIAL was dedicated on Memorial Day, May 30th, 1922. Six weeks prior, an African American teacher in Washington, D.C. wrote to the chairman of the Lincoln Memorial Commission who happened to be a justice sitting on the Supreme Court, former United States President, William Howard Taft. The teacher asked the question, "Should not someone prominent of the African American race speak at the dedication of the Lincoln Memorial?" At the 11th hour, the Lincoln Memorial Commission reached out to Dr. Robert Moton of the Tuskegee Institute. He was the successor to Booker T. Washington.

Moton was similar to Lincoln in many ways. He was an accommodationist and a mild-mannered person with which the commission could easily work. People believed that he would not say anything radical or inflammatory. Moton was invited to speak on the condition that he had to submit all of his public remarks before the dedication for review and approval. In essence, even though Moton was viewed as mild, he was being censored.

Moton would be the first of three keynote speakers. He decided to go off the script and suggested that Lincoln's most significant accomplishment was not the preservation of the Union but having the moral courage to end slavery. What Moton recognized was that ninety-nine percent of the symbolism built into the Lincoln Memorial honored one of Lincoln's significant accomplishments at the expense of another. In the wake of the First World War, the memorial was principally constructed as a symbol of national strength and unity. The inscription above Lincoln reads, "In this temple / As in the hearts of the people / For whom he saved the Union / The memory of Abraham Lincoln / Is enshrined forever." The inscription only mentions preservation of the Union. Nowhere is there any mention that Lincoln dared to end slavery. Most likely today there would be a summary inscription combining both accomplishments, not just one. African American citizens clearly saw this favoritism, which played up Lincoln as the savior of the Union and downplayed Lincoln as an emancipator. This message would change the sentiment at the memorial. What was once a place of reflection and contemplation was evolving into a reminder of the racial division that still existed. The symbolism would catalyze a shift in the way the Lincoln Memorial would be used.

When the day of the dedication came, Moton challenged the explicit message carved on the stone of the memorial and suggested that Lincoln's most significant accomplishment was the emancipation of slavery. At the ceremony were prominent Washington, D.C. African American lawyers, attorneys, and professors from Howard University. Upon arriving before the ceremony, they were shown to their segregated black only seating area far down the plaza in a position where it was difficult to hear. The Marines and the ushers mistreated them as they were shown to their seats. This caused many of the notable African American attendees to leave in disgust before the ceremonies began. The African American press had a field day covering the dedication at the Lincoln Memorial. On May 30th, 1922, the Lincoln Memorial was officially open to the public, but was it fully representative of all people?

Easter Sunday of 1939 was warm and sunny. The White House had given Harold Ickes the blessing to allow Marion Anderson to perform her concert outdoors. She chose the steps of the Lincoln Memorial with a purpose. Anderson's concert was a game changing moment because of the fiasco concerning the dedication of the Lincoln Memorial. On that day, there was no segregated seating. Everyone was there to enjoy the voice of this iconic opera singer. At that moment, the Lincoln Memorial transcended all the symbolism that the original sculptor, artist, and architect of the memorial had intentionally left out.

The events of that day would make the Lincoln Memorial an

epicenter for discussing the state of the nation and what kind of country the citizens of the United States wanted for the future. Time has erased the dedication of 1922 from people's memories. Recordings and photography are not anywhere near what they would have been had this event happened decades later. Even in 1939, Marion Anderson's concert, as beautiful and inclusive as it was, was not adequately captured by media production. However, many demonstrations later, on the steps of the Lincoln Memorial, at nearly the same place that Robert Morton stood on the day of the Lincoln Memorial dedication, a reverend named Dr. Martin Luther King Jr. would be recorded. With the advent of audio and video recordings, the way an event was remembered and memorialized was becoming much more accurate. The events of the early years of the Lincoln Memorial are a stark reminder that people need to understand that the historical recollection of people and events can be inaccurate, and some events can even be forgotten entirely. Recorded history is often as much about the historian as the event itself.

(4)

DOES HISTORY OR circumstance choose who is memorialized? Three years after the Lincoln Memorial was completed, a spot south of the Washington Monument on the Tidal Basin would be designated as the last great spot for a possible memorial in the nation's front yard. In 1925, Congress authorized the creation of the Theodore Roosevelt Memorial Commission. However, today there is no large monument in Washington, D.C. dedicated to Theodore Roosevelt.

The Theodore Roosevelt Memorial Commission held an open design competition for their potential monument. They hired a public relations firm to push their plans, raise funds, and expand public interest. They even declared a winner and gave the winning architect the $25,000 cash prize that they had offered. They had considerable steam, but ultimately, the idea of giving Teddy Roosevelt the final place of honor in the nation's front yard went down in flames for three key reasons. First, Teddy Roosevelt had only been dead for six years. Thomas Jefferson had been dead for over a century. It was too soon for Roosevelt, and it was Jefferson's turn. Second, if the country had built this Roosevelt Memorial, political scholars would argue that there are two Republican presidential monuments and none for the Democrats. Democrats were entirely enthusiastic to get that final place of honor. The third strike came when Roosevelt's wife came out in opposition to this monument being built only six years after Roosevelt's death. She worried that the family might be perceived as being too self-centered. The widow of Theodore Roosevelt had no choice but to say, "Thank you, but no thank you."

When Democrat Franklin Roosevelt moved into the White House in 1933, it was a high priority project of the FDR administration to make sure that Jefferson got that final spot of honor. The Jefferson Memorial was built by FDR and his Democratic party as a counterpoint to the Lincoln Memorial, which represented the Republican party. The original plans for a Jefferson Memorial called for a gigantic memorial to be built directly in the middle of where the Tidal Basin is today, with the memorial climbing twenty feet higher than the Lincoln Memorial. The Democrats' plan was to outdo the Republicans with their new memorial. At this point, the memories of both Jefferson's and Lincoln's legacies were utterly disregarded; instead of honoring the former presidents, it had become all about the strength and representation of the two political parties. This was political one-upmanship at its finest. If the plan for this gargantuan Jefferson Memorial had been completed, the whole Tidal Basin would have had to be redesigned. There was one more issue. Though everyone knew that the building of this monument would change the face of Washington, D.C., no one was more protective of the Japanese cherry trees than the women of Washington, D.C. Women took great pride in the trees because First Lady Taft and Viscountess Chinda, wife of the Japanese Ambassador, had planted the first trees together.

The women of Washington would not stand for a giant memorial to Thomas Jefferson at the expense of the cherry trees; in fact, they insisted that Jefferson himself would have stood arm-in-arm with them to protect the trees. There was such a tsunami of opposition about the plans of the Jefferson Memorial that it became the most contentious memorial project the country had ever seen. Not only was the size of the monument and the location a threat to the Japanese cherry trees, but the commission in charge of the project had also decided to use classical Roman architecture for the memorial. In the 1930s, Roman architecture was considered to be deader than the dinosaurs. Everything in the 1930s was about modern art and modern architecture. Frank Lloyd Wright famously called the potential design for the Jefferson Memorial an arrogant insult to the memory of Thomas Jefferson. Washington had every example of Roman architecture with numerous structures and buildings built in that style. Many people questioned why the commission would build yet another memorial in the overused Roman architectural style.

Roosevelt realized that to appeal to the general public, a different architectural style would have to be used. Roosevelt, like Jefferson, saw himself as an amateur architect. He knew a little bit about what he was talking about. He used his influence to have the Jefferson Memorial be built by a landscape architect, rather than a traditional architect. This was a turning point in the monument's construction. The concept was to build a memorial to be a place that was more open to the air and would add an element of education.

Memorials tend to say less about whom they are memorializing and more about the generation of people that are building them. The Washington Monument had been completed in 1885. Americans were beating their chests because they had constructed the tallest human-made structure ever built. It was not a statement about George Washington; instead, America was making a statement that they were becoming a player on the world scene. Just a few years later, the French put Americans in their place with the construction of the Eiffel Tower. The Washington Monument is 555 feet tall, and when the Eiffel Tower construction reached 556 feet, Gustave Eiffel took a timeout to party with his workmen to celebrate the fact that they now had the tallest structure in the world. The Eiffel Tower would eventually be completed and stand 1,063 feet tall.

(5)

UNLESS A PERSON gives a firsthand account of their experience with a famous person or a historical event, the odds of misrepresentation increase. Even with firsthand accounts, people's biases and personal views will influence what is written down. Why does history get so distorted?

It would be nice to believe that all historians do not have hidden agendas. Likewise, when a monument is constructed, the hope would be that the monument accurately depicts the person or event it memorializes. As with the Lincoln Memorial, the Jefferson Memorial, and the Washington Monument, those involved in designing and building them often reveal more about themselves than they do about the people or events that they are supposed to be memorializing. The further an event is from the present day, the larger the distortion of history can be. At some point, the people who can give firsthand accounts will be gone, and then people must rely on secondhand accounts. The description of history is almost like a game of telephone. In telephone, children sit in a line, and the first child is given a phrase on a notecard. That child whispers the phrase to the person next to them, who then whispers the message to the next child, and so on and so forth. The phrase that the final child says to the group is almost never the same as what is on the notecard. The description of history is like playing telephone; human understanding and biases cause the "phrase" to continually change over time.

It is impossible to represent the past with 100 percent accuracy since most of the time, the presenters were not there. This can skew reality. Sometimes there is an intentional misrepresentation because of an ulterior motive. In the case of the Jefferson Memorial, a tribute to Jefferson was decided upon because there was a perception that two Republican monuments would dominate the lack of representation for the Democrats. Likewise, the placements of the inscriptions on the Lincoln memorial favor Lincoln, the Savior of the Union at the expense of Lincoln, the Great Emancipator.

Dr. Joseph Warren was an American Patriot and physician living in colonial Boston. He was the president of the Massachusetts Provincial Congress that was one of the most active oppositions to British rule. When British army movements suggested the possibility of troop activities, Joseph Warren asked Paul Revere to take a horse and warn the Massachusetts Provincial Congress in Concord. This was the site of one of the larger caches of the colonial rebels' arms and ammunition; also in Concord were the Patriot leaders John Hancock and Samuel Adams. Revere's job was to give early warning to the Patriots in Concord and Lexington. On the evening of April 18th, 1775, Paul Revere, a silversmith, left his home in Boston to ride through the town of Lexington yelling, "The British are coming! The British are coming!" It is a story ingrained in American folklore, and since it has made its way into the teaching of history, most people do not question what Paul Revere did. The whole story never happened.

How did Paul Revere gain the reputation for having saved many colonists by riding through the night yelling, "The British are coming?" In 1860, eighty-five years after the start of the American Revolution, Henry Wadsworth Longfellow wrote the poem

"Paul Revere's Ride." It was published in January of 1861 in the Boston magazine, *The Atlantic Monthly*. Longfellow imagined the events of April 18th, 1775 as he climbed to the Old North Church in Boston where lanterns were lit to signal, *one if by land, two if by sea*. The day after Longfellow visited the church, he wrote about Paul Revere's ride. Longfellow was an abolitionist, and at the time that he wrote this poem, the American Civil War was about to erupt. Significant inaccuracies in Longfellow's writing attributed the lighting of the lanterns in the church to Revere, when Revere simply gave the orders for the lanterns. Longfellow also depicted Revere riding alone, but he was one of at least three riders. Revere was joined by William Dawes, William Prescott, and possibly more men that were never recorded. British soldiers stopped all three men. Dawes and Prescott escaped, while Revere was detained by the British and taken back to Boston.

Longfellow's poems portray history based on his romanticism with rebellion. Longfellow wanted to see a country free of slavery. He created an inaccurate depiction of history when he wrote about Paul Revere, and ironically, his version of complete fiction stuck. At the turn of the 20th century, J.P. Morgan would pay $100,000 for a punch bowl that Paul Revere had made. Morgan was not buying the punch bowl because he valued Paul Revere, the silversmith; he was infatuated with Paul Revere, the horseback rider. Longfellow had created all this allure.

What really happened at this point in history? The British would enter Concord and Lexington, marking the start of the American Revolutionary War. Dr. Joseph Warren would reach the rank of Major General in the colonial militia. With his rank, it was not necessary for him to engage in battle; he was supposed to give orders instead. Warren was not this type of man. He thrived on overcoming challenges. When Warren arrived at Bunker Hill, he asked General Israel Putnam where he thought the heaviest fighting would be. Putnam indicated that he believed the most significant challenge would be on Breed's Hill. Against the will of both William Prescott and Putnam, Warren entered the battle, taking on the rank of a lieutenant. Prescott and Putnam wanted Warren to serve as their commander at the battle, but Warren believed that his skills were best utilized by forcing troops to hold a line under distress. After three assaults by the British on Breed's Hill, Warren would remain as one of the final Patriots holding off the British Army, allowing many of the militia to escape before he was killed.

Paul Revere, Israel Putnam, and William Prescott would all live beyond the Revolutionary War. They would be remembered. Dr. Joseph Warren would be less remembered. Even so, two reminders still exist. First, his family commissioned artist John Trumbull to paint *The Death of General Warren at Bunker Hill, June 17, 1775*. Trumbull's *Declaration of Independence, Surrender of General Burgoyne, Surrender of Lord Cornwallis,* and *General George Washington Resigning His Commission* all hang in the rotunda of the United States Capital. Because Warren's death was captured by Trumbull's art, which is iconic, he is in part remembered. Secondly, a statue of Dr. Joseph Warren is housed in an exhibit area adjacent to Bunker Hill. Most accounts of the Battle of Bunker Hill state that Prescott may never have uttered his famous words. In fact, according to author Robert Earnest Hubbard, the phrase, "Don't fire until you see the whites of their eyes," was most likely said by someone other than Prescott, or possibly no one at all.

Paul Revere's ride and Abraham Lincoln's Monument capture the mindsets of builders, politicians, society, and writers. Historically, they are examples of the many inaccurate depictions of history seen through the eyes of those who lived years later. History is written the way people want it to look. Even Abraham Lincoln was not immune.

This chapter began with an interview with Jahana Hayes. Though Hayes revealed information about a teacher she disliked and a counselor that went out of her way to help her, the interview disclosed a lot about Hayes herself. She is a United States Congresswoman and a National Teacher of the Year. She nearly dropped out of high school. Had Hayes dropped out, she never would have reached this incredible level of distinction. Though her resume has achievements that few can compare to, I would argue that the greatest accomplishment of Hayes' life has been overcoming real life challenges. Certainly, Hayes will be remembered, but will it be for her accomplishments or her ability to rise above adversity? Hayes' story parallels many of the people that are memorialized in Washington. Most memorials commemorate the accomplishment, not the conviction, of the individual. Hayes' interview reminds us that it is important to value people for the way they live their life as much, or possibly more, than single achievements.

# Interview with Randall McDaniel
*January 6, 2019*
*San Francisco, California*

*I met Randall McDaniel when I was with the National Teacher of the Year program. We were at an evening event the night before the 2019 College Football National Championship. McDaniel played pro football as an offensive guard for the Minnesota Vikings and the Tampa Bay Buccaneers. In 2009, he was inducted as a member of the National Football Hall of Fame.*

**Albrecht:** I'm here with Randall McDaniel. How would you define yourself?

**McDaniel:** How would I define myself? A person out there in the world trying to make a difference a little bit, trying to give back to the community as much as they have given me. It's hard to say... a person who cares about others, a person who cares about what is going on in the world, a person who wants to always get better and help people find those paths that they can channel.

**Albrecht:** So, Randall, let me ask you this, who was your favorite teacher? First, how old are you?

**McDaniel:** Fifty-four.

**Albrecht:** OK, fifty-four. Who's your favorite teacher?

**McDaniel:** I have two. My third-grade teacher, Mrs. Pyle. That was Aberdale Elementary School. She is no longer with us, but I got a chance to go back and thank her for keeping me inside for recess back in the day to get work done. And, then my high school mentor who I still do stuff with now, O.K. Fulton.

**Albrecht:** What high school?

**McDaniel:** Agua Fria High School. He was a person who came to me and said that he wanted to know the young man, not the athlete, and then from eighth grade on until I graduated and went to college, he has been in my life. He actually presented me at the Hall of Fame. That is whom I had as my friend and mentor. So, those were my two favorites right there.

**Albrecht:** So, you really did love school?

**McDaniel:** They made that difference for me when I was going to school where at that time, I needed someone to step in and say, "You can do it," and they did. And so, all my friends were teachers going to college and everything. It is a simple thing to do. No one's beaten up on the body before, but I get asked what is the toughest, playing football against those NFL linemen or working in a school, and I go, football was easy. Working with those kids, you really got that challenge. I love that challenge.

**Albrecht:** Have you ever coached?

**McDaniel:** No. They try to get me to coach every year and come in the high school. The hard part is, my own opinion, the coaching part would be the easy part. Dealing with the parents is hard. It all comes with the baggage.

**Albrecht:** OK, three words to describe Mrs. Pyle?

**McDaniel:** Oh, you really hit me… Mrs. Pyle. Outstanding. Loyal. And, someone like she was like family to me.

**Albrecht:** And, your high school teacher?

**McDaniel:** Mr. Fulton?

**Albrecht:** Yes.

**McDaniel:** Father. It is hard to describe someone in three words... great role model. Hell of a mentor. And, overall, I can't say a good friend. I can say a good family.

### Reflection:

In my teacher world, spring is spelling bee season. I do not watch much television in the evenings, but for two days, I stay glued to the TV watching the Howard-Scripps National Spelling Bee. Each year it is held in Washington, D.C. with students from all over the United States. The winner walks away with $25,000 and National Spelling Bee fame. Many contestants have their own set of rituals, patterns, and some quirks. For one moment each year, a trophy is raised in victory on ESPN that has very little to do with physical achievement. Spelling bees are about cognitive talent and a lot of studying, right?

In 2001, a fourth grader of mine named Christian reported on a current event to our class about the National Spelling Bee. He was a talented speller and suggested that we should have a school-wide spelling bee. The school I teach in has a fourth and fifth grade. Students who qualify for the National Spelling Bee must be under fourteen years of age. Christian decided that our school should try to identify a champion, have them compete at the regional competition, and send them to Washington, D.C. The number of contestants has changed, but approximately 250 students are invited to the National Spelling Bee each year. In 2002, the Democrat and Chronicle newspaper of Rochester, New York, underwrote the regional competition in our area.

Christian was adamant; we needed to have a spelling bee. The following year, with his help, I organized the first spelling bee in our school's history. We divided the event into two spelling bees by grade level, and the school bought dictionaries for the top five spellers at each grade. After much planning, I was sure that this was going to be a fantastic event for the community and the school. The top spellers were going to be sponsored by the PTSA to be entered in the county spelling bee. We identified two students from every classroom to compete. Everything looked positive.

Here are some statistics from the spelling bee in year number one: seven kids left the stage crying. One student threw up. Two students decided at the last minute to quit, and we only had dictionaries to look up the words. Students can ask for a definition or a sentence. There was no internet in the cafeteria, so electronic dictionaries were not possible. If a student asked for a word's definition, the judges had to look it up manually in a book dictionary. It was slow and painful. After year number one, the thought of a second spelling bee looked dismal. At the regional spelling bee, our top finisher came in 89th out of 120.

As Ralph Waldo Emmerson once said, "Every artist was once an amateur." Schools, teachers, and students do not always get it right on the first try, because education is both an art and a science. The science of education means that educators and students need to observe every experience and make changes if necessary. We need people who can stay the course when opportunities fall apart. A teacher who understands the art of teaching is better equipped to understand what they observe. Hypothetically, a person could walk into an art gallery and look at an extraordinary piece of art and call it beautiful, but do they truly understand why the piece they are looking at is extraordinary? If that person has worked in the medium of art that they are observing then, yes, they may understand the incredible skill set of the artist. However, if the person observing the art has never created art, will they truly understand the artwork's complexity?

A master teacher needs to be an artist. Each student has the potential to be his or her own masterpiece, but the guidance of a teacher is the catalyst for this to happen. No two people on the planet are identical, so the artistic nature of a teacher is the ability to see the strengths and weaknesses of every person, often with over thirty students in a room, and give each student what they need to develop. Even in a spelling bee, each student is different and needs a teacher who can identify what each individual needs proactively, within the moment, and after the moment has passed. For a teacher to be able to do this, there is a high level of artistic ability within their skill set.

Randall McDaniel talked about how Mrs. Pyle kept him accountable at recess so he could keep pace with what was expected of him academically. Randall was getting a lot of play time after school. She had to decide. What was more valuable, recess or learning? For each student, this may be different. It seems ironic that an athlete would love a third-grade teacher that took recess away to help him maintain an academic pace with his classmates. His interview shows that a teacher needs to make decisions based on the individual. Almost fifty years later, McDaniel remembered the teacher that saw what he needed. In McDaniel's memory, a teacher that preached work ethic had a significant impact on his life.

Later in Randall McDaniel's interview, he remembered Mr. Fulton. He stopped himself when he was going to call Mr. Fulton a friend, and he replaced friend with family. As McDaniel stated, "Mr. Fulton wanted to get to know the young man, not just the football player." McDaniel is in the National Football Hall of Fame, and yet his second beloved teacher is a person who wanted to know him beyond the playing field. McDaniel's statement indicates that some people may have needs that are masked by their talent. I would infer that this is the reason McDaniel has never coached football. Instead, he serves others by identifying what people need to be successful.

After a few years of struggle, the spelling bee morphed. The talent pool did not change, but the approach of our school did. We recognized that talent does not guarantee confidence and a healthy self-concept. Like Mrs. Pyle, we identified what each student needed to grow. In Randall McDaniel's case, he needed to be held in at recess for additional instruction. In the case of the spelling bee contestants, they needed to know how to handle their emotions. Every student is different. We began to have four practice sessions before the spelling bee, and we talked about how emotions can be challenged. For many of these keen academic students, they had never faced academic failure. The spelling bee was no longer about spelling words correctly. Instead, we stopped worrying about spelling and began teaching resilience in the face of failure. Like Mr. Fulton, we got to know each person and worried about the child rather than the spelling bee contestant. By making personal connections, academically talented students learned how to control their emotions. We have a teacher that presents each student with a t-shirt when they are eliminated for misspelling a word. She is well-versed in helping students understand their feelings in the face of disappointment. Now in its 19th year, the Hill School Spelling Bee is a highly anticipated event. People from all over the community come to watch.

In 1975, the United States passed Public Law 94-142. The Education for All Handicapped Children Act required all public schools accepting federal funds to provide equal access to education and one free meal a day for children with physical and mental disabilities. Public schools were required to evaluate children with disabilities and create an educational plan with parent input that would provide, as closely as possible, the educational experience of non-disabled students. The law helps level the playing field for disabled students through an educational plan. However, I would argue that this plan does not go far enough. After a quarter of a century in education, I have yet to meet a student that does not have some need. The needs may not require formalization on a document like they do for students with disabilities, but the demands of the curriculum can create blindness for the recognition of the individual needs of students. Personal relationships between teachers and students are the most underrated effort in education, and it is one of the most crucial factors for guiding students to become successful. Randall McDaniel had needs, and Mrs. Pyle was there to make sure his educational needs were met. Mr. Fulton recognized the need for a father figure. If these teachers did not identify McDaniel's needs, would he have become a Hall of Fame football player? Randall McDaniel's memories of Mrs. Pyle and Mr. Fulton remind us that building relationships between students and teachers is essential to understanding the unique needs of all students.

## Chapter 8
## Noah's Boat Was Round:
## History, Its Writers & Who Really Matters

(1)

April 15th, 2015 was a Wednesday. This date is likely insignificant to most people. On that day, three events took place. In New York State, springtime in schools is the state testing season. Front and center on the cover of most newspapers across the state of New York was a statistical breakdown of parents who decided to opt their children out of state testing. There was turmoil over the undefined impact test data would have on teachers and students. Most newspapers sensationalize what the news of the day is, and what could have been a fantastic story was missed. That particular year, many families were concerned about how the states that were administering standardized tests were using student test data. People also had concerns over the level of appropriateness for having such high stakes tests being used with children.

On April 15th, 1947, the first African American baseball player stepped onto a major league baseball field. His name was Jackie Robinson. By coincidence, on April 15th, 1865 President Abraham Lincoln was assassinated, becoming the first American President to be killed while in office. These two events were pivotal moments in American history. They were overshadowed and did not make front page stories on their anniversaries. 2015 was the

150th anniversary of Lincoln's assassination. There are few more notable people and refernced moments than April 15th, 1865. What happened? The news media forgot about honoring the life of service that Lincoln led, and that day was overshadowed with protests about state testing. Though the state testing headlines of April 15th, 2015 may have sold more newspapers, there was social blindness to the commemoration of great history.

What is the best way to serve others? The system of service in modern America looks a lot different than it did a century ago. There is an evident and apparent shift on how service to one another is performed. Society has become project oriented with assigned times to tasks. Donations increase during specific seasons, even though there is a need year-round, and most community service is taught by accumulating hours toward a service goal. Is this living a life of service? Because of people's busy lives, service has become one of those one-shot deals. Boy Scouts do park cleanups, a day at a nursing home, and canned food drives. All these activities are good, aren't they? These projects often make newspaper headlines that read something like "Mr. Smith's Class Raised $250 for the Red Cross." Philanthropy mimics this standardization as well. Pure philanthropy takes about as much work as it took to make money in the first place. Philanthropy done right ensures that the project that is started continues for years to come. The money must be carefully watched and managed. A one-shot deal makes headlines, too, but does it sustain growth? Like the pre-scheduled lives many people are leading, service to others has been compartmentalized; it is measured in hours or dollars. On

April 15th, 2015, a hot topic, state testing, was pasted corner to corner on the front of most major newspapers. The reality is that nobody will remember this headline years from now. Even with the intensity of the debate, this headline will fade in our memories.

For Abraham Lincoln, the Civil War and his presidency were about the way he viewed humanity. Lincoln lived a life of service and conviction. Most likely he would have been fine laying down his life for his beliefs. Lincoln died at fifty-six years old, but his impact changed the course of American history. In his own words: "In the end, it's not the years in your life that count. It is the life in your years." Lincoln led a lifelong crusade to fulfill his belief that all men are created equal. In 1858, he agreed to debate the topic of slavery with Stephen Douglass to win the Illinois Senate seat. Lincoln lost that election, but a life of service means that, win or lose, perseverance in the face of obstacles is what matters most. He would become President of the United States in 1860. On April 15th, 2015, this was all forgotten. Wins and losses do not matter to a person that is living by the moral standards to which they have devoted their lives.

April 15th is celebrated each year by Major League Baseball as Jackie Robinson Day. Like Lincoln, Robinson was committed to his cause. He was chosen to be the first person of color to have this opportunity because he was talented, and he lived a life of non-violence. He could tolerate the barrage of bigotry and the angry anti-black protesters that threatened his life. Robinson continued to live life to help promote equal rights. After his playing career, he became the first black vice president of a major American corporation, Chock Full o'Nuts. He also helped establish the Freedom National Bank. The first of its kind, Freedom National Bank was an African American-owned financial institution based in New York City. Robinson lived a life dedicated to the principles of equality. He did not stray far from Major League Baseball. After his playing years had passed, he became the first television analyst of color. Like Lincoln, on April 15th, 2015, Robinson's legacy was also brushed aside.

Strong emotions within the moment command headlines. Headlines do not consistently display the slow and steady stream of what has shaped our society. That day, people got so wrapped up in their busy lives that many failed to recognize the significance of history. A life of service has an enduring impact. Leaders living lives of service often do not make headlines because their focus is on steady progress, not individual moments. Does our media remember great people who changed the angle for which the world is headed and commemorate their contributions?

We preach that service is essential, but it is performed in blocks of convenient time. What shifts a society are not the headliners, but the people who choose to live lives of service. Their stories often live on the back pages of newspapers or go entirely unnoticed. On April 15th, 2015, what mattered? What events will have an enduring and everlasting impression on society as a whole? Newspapers had a choice on April 15th, 2015, and what they chose to publicize did have an effect on what everyone considered that day.

(2)

BERNARD CASEY CANNOT be found in the history books. Born to two farming Irish immigrants in 1870, he was sixth in a line of sixteen children. He grew up in the western section of Wisconsin, and at age eight contracted diphtheria, which permanently damaged his voice. Though he was small in stature, he left home at age seventeen to pursue a career as a lumberjack. It was a surprise to many who saw young Bernard as a rather weak and pitiful person. He bounced from job to job, becoming an orderly in a hospital, a Minnesota correctional officer, and a streetcar operator.

Casey had little to no vision for his life. Most people lead predictable lives, often developing their life vision because somewhere along the path of life, a person had an impact, which produced a spark of interest. Inspiration activates interest. This was not the young Bernard's circumstance.

Casey's spark finally came, but it was not a positive one. As a streetcar driver, he witnessed a brutal murder. Bearing witness to this brutality shifted Casey's life to find its purpose. He decided to devote his life to a higher order of peace. In 1892, Bernard Casey was admitted to a German seminary, but due to his lack of education, the seminarians did not believe he possessed the ability to become a priest. His poor schooling and the German-English language barrier obstructed his goals. His superiors deemed Casey unable to succeed.

In 1896, a discouraged Casey left the German seminary and entered a Capuchin institute. The Capuchin friars are recognizable by their brown Franciscan robes, always with a cap or hood. They live in simplicity and do not collect a salary. They forego the possession of money and only own essential items. While in seminary with the Capuchin, Casey changed his name to Solanus. Though it cannot be confirmed, he most likely changed his name as a follower of Francis Solanus, a Spanish missionary from the 16th and 17th centuries. Francis Solanus was not physically robust, but he possessed a spiritual mind, which allowed him to communicate and develop relationships, some of which were with natives of Peru living on the western coast of North America.

Solanus Casey was ordained as a simplex priest, meaning that he could not hear confessions or bless the Eucharist, but he could hold the title of a priest. Oddly in 1957, this man of little education, so little that the church would not grant him full priesthood, would have 20,000 people pay tribute to him upon his death. Pope John Paul II would also name him as venerable, the last step to achieving sainthood. He was the first American to be given this recognition. This is the same man who was discarded by so many at a young age. After his death, Casey was exhumed and reburied in the Saint Bonaventure Monastery in Detroit.

Casey dedicated his life to service. People waited in line to talk to him. He had multiple assignments near and in New York City, including duties at Sacred Heart Friary in Yonkers, Saint John the Baptist Church near Penn Station, and as time passed, Our Lady of Angels Church in Harlem. The final twenty-one years of his life were spent at St. Bonaventure Monastery in Detroit, Michigan. He was a receptionist and a doorkeeper. Casey was given jobs of little value. Rather than let his circumstances pull him down, Casey defined his own value. Casey fully committed to a complete life of service. He lived an uncomplicated life and devoted all he could to the full attention of the people in his presence, one person at a time. Who were his people? The destitute and the sick came to Solanus Casey for inspiration, consultation, and healing. He spent most of his time, often one on one, with people who were forgotten like him. A growing number of people began attending his Wednesday services for the sick. Many saw his extraordinary compassion and were amazed at how helpful his consultations were. With no scientific explanation, after consulting with Casey, many sick people gained their health back.

Miraculous or merely inspirational, Solanus Casey, a weak and undereducated man, was being considered for sainthood. Why? He did not own a business or even possessions. He did not invent anything or lead a nation, but he did devote his life to a service that fit his abilities. For that, the Catholic Church considers him worthy to be placed on the path leading to sainthood. Much like Abraham Lincoln and Jackie Robinson, Casey served in a way that fit who he was. He accepted his role and limitations, and he contributed what he could. He was not intended to lead a sizeable humanitarian movement like Lincoln or command a patriot rebellion like Washington. Solanus Casey was destined to consult with people. He did this and was honest with himself. His acknowledgment of his abilities guided his service, and that made a difference.

This chapter began with an interview with NFL Hall of Famer, Randall McDaniel. McDaniel shared how a coach had an unconventional and enduring impact on his life. McDaniel was introduced at the National Football Hall of Fame by his high school coach, O.K. Fulton. Why did McDaniel select him? Fulton was interested in McDaniel as a person, not just as a football player. Like Solanus Casey, Fulton devoted time to McDaniel because he cared for him. It led to a lifelong friendship and an overwhelming sense of Fulton being part of McDaniel's family. Had Fulton only interacted with McDaniel as a player, it would be analogous to a one-shot community service project. An on the field interaction may have had some effect, but full impact occurs when longevity and commitment in the interests of others becomes the priority.

What role does spiritual development play in the soul of a human being? Casey's association with the Catholic Church influenced a large segment of the local people by the way that he conducted his life and the example he set. Each person is different. For some, spiritual development is more critical than for others. Religion, whether it is essential to an individual or not, has to be acknowledged as a defining factor for the development of societies, families, and individuals.

Regular spiritual practice is a form of service. It is difficult for people to recognize spiritualism as a form of service because its practice is almost exclusively exercised in private homes or churches, at least in the United States. It is commonplace to say *I will pray for them*, when referring to the sick. Alternatively, when someone has died, the card that is sent to the deceased member's family often includes a message such as *we are praying for you*. For people of faith, praying for another human being is akin to service, and the development of spirituality increases the odds for success.

Religious affiliation is not essential to this spiritual sense if it has an impact on the participants.

Thomas Jefferson's advocacy for the separation of church and state made religion a private matter. Though religious history can be studied in public schools, spiritual development and formalized religion cannot be practiced. The thirteen original English colonies did not have a separation of church and state, though the roots of public schools in the United States reach back into the Colonial Era. In 1647, the Old Deluder Act or Satan Deluder Act was passed by the Massachusetts Bay Colony. This was the first educational law established in the British Colonies. It called for a school to be built in every township having over fifty homes. The motivation behind this law was the belief that Satan was hindering people from learning the Christian scriptures. To ensure the preservation of good and the will of God, the government created a public school system. Jefferson would be the first to advocate for the separation of church and state. He argued that religious matters are personal and should be guided by the individual. This jammed a wedge between the government and organized religion.

According to the Search Institute, a belief in God or gods and an affiliation to a religious organization increases the probability of a successful life. How do we develop these assets in a publicly funded system? Since religion is a personal choice, the empowerment of students needs to be emphasized, so each student may build their spiritual belief on their own.

(3)

IN DECEMBER OF 2003, the 100th anniversary of the Wright brothers' man-powered flight was celebrated in Kill Devil Hills, North Carolina. In 1903, the area was called Kitty Hawk, but the towns have been since rezoned, and now the famous hill resides in Kill Devil Hills. The town's name comes from moonshiners who lived on the far side of the hill that the Wright brothers used for their first flights; their moonshine was said to *kill the devil*. In December of 2003, there was a full week of celebration, exhibits, and presentations recognizing the milestone of the advent of aviation. Under a rain-filled sky, Buzz Aldrin and Neil Armstrong delivered remarks about the historical significance of the event and how it led America to be pioneers as the first and only country to send people to the moon.

*We traveled to the moon.* The word *we* is often used when people talk about this pioneering voyage, which spanned over 280,000 miles. The mission bound a nation together and inspired Americans to feel a sense of unified accomplishment.

Though NASA packed most of the essential equipment for the journeys of all the space missions, the Apollo astronauts were allowed to bring some small personal items. The capsule they would travel in was smaller than the interior of an economy car. Did Neil Armstrong, Buzz Aldrin, and Michael Collins argue over what flavor of Pringles to take? Perhaps this question sounds foolish, but it is realistic. What did they bring? Most of the astronauts brought along pictures of their families, which they left on the moon. Astronauts were allowed to take a cassette tape of their favorite music, which incidentally was unanimously country music.

NASA is funded publicly and is budgeted federally. Its financial stability is never on permanently secure ground. If schools cannot hold religious practice, are religious practices at NASA, which is funded by the public, any different? In the years preceding the Apollo 11 lunar landing, proclaimed atheist Madalyn Murray O'Hair maintained an ongoing watch of NASA. It was O'Hair who is best known for the Murray vs. Curlett lawsuit that led to the end of Bible reading in American schools. In 1969, O'Hair recognized that the Apollo 11 moon mission would be the perfect backdrop for a devout Presbyterian to synthesize God with this historic moment. Though O'Hair did not represent mainstream America, to avoid confrontation, NASA asked Armstrong, Aldrin, and Collins to refrain from quoting the Bible while on the Apollo 11 mission. Contrary to the directive that NASA issued, Aldrin did bring something of spiritual value along with him to the moon: communion.

With all of the public eyes watching, quietly Buzz Aldrin took blessed bread and wine to the moon. Aldrin is a Presbyterian by faith. Though July 20th, 1969 marks the date in which a man walked on the moon, it also marks the day in which the first man celebrated Christian communion somewhere other than on Earth. The story first appeared in August of 1969 in *Life Magazine*, and then was reported in an October 1970 article in *Guideposts*. In 2009, Aldrin published his book, *Magnificent Desolation*, in which he chronicled the moment as well. Neil Armstrong respectfully watched, but he did not participate. By coincidence, July 20th, 1969 was a Sunday.

Buzz Aldrin was a reverent man. He celebrated communion 280,000 miles away from Earth, alone. Later, he reported that drinking communion wine out of a bag was a challenge. The bread was broken from a loaf from his home church. According to the schedule NASA had given Armstrong and Aldrin, seven hours after landing on the moon the astronauts were supposed to eat, rest, sleep, and collect their thoughts. Mission Control communicated this downtime to the media. Aldrin saw this as the perfect time, out of the view of the world, for a private celebration of Christian gratitude. He had consulted with his pastor, Dean Woodruff, looking for a patriotic gesture to do in preparation for that historical moment of the lunar landing, but after speaking with the pastor, Aldrin settled on communion.

Why did Buzz Aldrin choose to do this? Great leaders stay true to what is meaningful to them. This honesty is defined by every individual, whether they agree or disagree with other people's thoughts. Why not just take a nap? Does it matter what is done in private? Does this define a person? Absolutely. Though men like Abraham Lincoln, Buzz Aldrin, and a lesser-known Solanus Casey lived in the public eye, their private lives gave the most honest glimpse into what they believed. What is done in private serves people as much as what is done in public. The foundation for a house cannot be seen; it is under the ground. Without a foundation, a house will fall in a short time. Private moments are a foundation. Did Buzz Aldrin's celebration of communion change the world? Not visibly, but his private world provided the foundation for worldly success. His pattern of devoted service aligns with that of Solanus Casey and Abraham Lincoln.

(4)

ON JULY 29TH, 1958, President Dwight D. Eisenhower signed the NASA bill (S-3609), which established the National Aeronautics and Space Administration. Eisenhower had no interest in a space program, but he was under tremendous public pressure. America was falling behind the Soviet Union in the space race. The United States was stunned when Sputnik, a Soviet Satellite, was the first successful satellite to be put into orbit. The Soviets had moved ahead of the United States in the space race. This was followed by Uri Gagarin, a cosmonaut, becoming the first human in space. Suddenly, pride had a higher priority than domestic spending. By 1962, NASA's budget accounted for approximately 1.2% of all federal spending. This is a large and considerable investment. How does a proposal to create a new civilian and government-controlled agency amount to such a sizeable budgetary expense? From a financial standpoint, creating NASA was a gutsy move.

In an inconspicuous space in the National Museum of the United States Air Force is a steel balloon gondola. An argument could be made that it contains as much historical aviation significance as the Apollo 11 lunar lander. Behind it is a sign that reads Manhigh II Ballock Gondola. It is easy to walk right by this silver pill-shaped capsule without understanding the importance of the Manhigh Missions. The men who rode in this capsule are just as easy to ignore, despite their contributions to the United States. The names of Joseph Kittinger, David Simons, and Clifton McClure are not recognizable. However, their grit would set the standard for the Apollo astronauts.

In November of 1957, President Eisenhower had a significant challenge to tackle. With the October news of Sputnik, the United States was behind in the space race. The Sputnik satellite measured only 23 inches in diameter. Even if it was the size of a bus, it did not matter. Sputnik was the first. This was followed in November by a second Soviet satellite. The launching of two orbiting satellites was not only an issue of security, but being first also became a subject of national dignity. The satellites traveled at 17,500 miles per hour, which meant that they circled the Earth every ninety minutes, and each time it was orbiting right over the United States. Eisenhower was quick to appoint Dr. James R. Killian Jr., the president of the Massachusetts Institute of Technology, as his Special Assistant for Science and Technology. The Senate Preparedness Committee headed by Lyndon B. Johnson met immediately. They found that the American scientists working on rocketry systems, directed by Dr. Wernher von Braun, had asked for help in 1955. Their requests and plans had mostly been ignored. Von Braun had tried numerous times to get the go-ahead for a rocket launch, claiming that a rocket could be ready to go in 90 days. Still, he was ignored. Seventy-three witnesses provided their assessment of the United States missile technology and interpretations of the progress and events leading up to the launch of Sputnik. At the time, rocketry was explicitly under the oversight and operation of the military.

Project Vanguard had been working on rocket technology through the Navy, but they were unsuccessful at launching a satellite into orbit. John Hagan, NASA's Assistant Director of Space Flight, told Senator Lyndon B. Johnson that Project Vanguard could have beat Sputnik into space if it had been given a higher priority level. He reported that he had asked for the project to be granted more resources multiple times, but his superiors had always ignored his requests. Senator Johnson's Senate task force concluded that the Eisenhower White House had not allocated the funds, interest, or resources to make Vanguard a successful program. A visual and obvious exclamation point was put at the end of this conclusion when a United States Vanguard TV3 rocket lifted about three feet off the ground before coming right back down, resulting in a fiery explosion. Now that all of this was in the public eye, Eisenhower had to act. He did not. Eisenhower was set on staying ahead of the Soviets based on the ground military. Since space exploration was outside his vision of military supremacy, he perceived the exploration of space as a commercial venture. Eisenhower saw no use for a space program because he did not view its value as a form of national defense.

The National Advisory Committee for Aeronautics (NACA) was a United States federal agency founded on March 3rd, 1915 to undertake, promote, and institutionalize aeronautical research. It had not achieved its goal. In a speech on April 2nd, 1958 to a joint session of Congress, Eisenhower called for a civilian National Aeronautics and Space Agency (NASA). He handed down a directive ordering NACA and the Defense Department to begin arranging the transfer of nonmilitary projects and space assets within the Department of Defense to NASA. On April 14th, Lyndon Johnson and New Hampshire Republican Senator Styles Bridges introduced the Senate version of the NASA bill (S-3609), and Congressman John McCormack introduced the House version (HR-11881). Hearings commenced the following day.

On January 31st, 1958, the United States was finally able to get a satellite into orbit: the Explorer I. On May 1st, 1958, Dr. James Van Allen announced that high radiation levels had swamped radiation detectors aboard Explorer I and Explorer III (launched March 26th) at several points in their orbits. This showed the existence of powerful radiation belts surrounding the Earth. The detection of the Van Allen Belts was the first significant space discovery made in American history. The United States seemed to be making up ground.

The creation of NASA was a significant milestone for the United States. Within four years of its inception, the Americans had a man in orbit, and less than eleven years later, NASA was able to land a human-crewed space capsule on the moon. This displayed a revitalized commitment to engineering, determination, and forward thinking that the United States was now supporting. These achievements and the pioneering men and women who were part of the space program had accomplished something that no one would have dreamed of just a few decades before.

All military branches had a stake in the development of rocketry. Rockets are a crucial component of defensive and offensive war tactics. The Air Force had a compounded interest; much of Dr. Van Allen's work was a concern to the Air Force. Up to this point, nobody knew the answer to the questions surrounding the effects of cosmic radiation and rays on human beings.

At the time, Dr. John Strapp was working in New Mexico studying the effects of high acceleration and deceleration on humans. High altitude exploration interested Strapp, and as a result, he began Project Manhigh. The objective of Project Manhigh was to answer the questions of what effects high altitude, acceleration, and rapid deceleration would have on human beings. Instead of using rockets, Project Manhigh utilized helium balloons, which at maximum capacity and expansion extended to over a 200-foot diameter. A similar project, in which a man in a gondola reached an altitude of 51,788 feet, was executed in 1931 by the Swiss physicist Auguste Piccard.

On June 2nd, 1957, Captain Joseph Kittinger was launched by helium balloon into the stratosphere reaching an altitude of 96,784 feet. This was followed up a month later by a similar attempt in which Major David Simons lived in the stratosphere for thirty-two hours and reached an altitude exceeding 102,000 feet. Lieutenant Clifton Piccard would reach over 96,000 feet in the third and final mission. The knowledge gained by the Manhigh missions would pave the way for space exploration. In 1960, Joseph Kittinger would set the freefall skydiving record at 102,000 feet traveling at a maximum descent speed of 614 miles per hour. He lived.

With the 1958 inception of NASA, a lot of the work that the Air Force was managing, including project Manhigh, was shut down. Manhigh was not in the public's eye. NASA was. The new era of astronauts became the center of public interest, and people like Joseph Kittinger settled back into their military careers. Kittinger would go on to serve in the Vietnam War, where he earned a Silver Star. When Kittinger's plane was shot down over Vietnam in 1972, and he was a prisoner of war for the next eleven months, it did not make the front page of any newspaper in the country.

Fame and fortune were not on Captain Joseph Kittinger's priority list. Kittinger's desire to be the best when he was called upon and face a life-threatening challenge for the benefit of the advancement of humanity in flight and space is noble. He received many recognitions, but never to the extent that the Apollo astronauts did. His willingness to sacrifice himself allowed scientists to understand the outer reaches of Earth's stratosphere. The studies of David Simons' historic thirty-two-hour balloon flight gathered data that would help ensure the safety of the NASA astronauts.

Each human being can push the edge of what they do into uncharted territory. Without the willingness to do so, progress would never be achieved. When boundaries are stretched, new paths of discovery lead to success. It becomes the public's decision if a story is newsworthy. Failure to make headlines in the media should never negate the significance of competitive greatness.

(5)

DR. IRVING FINKEL is the assistant keeper of artifacts from the Middle East at the British History Museum in London. His inquisitive appearance and thick white beard may remind a person of Kris Kringle. He is a leading expert on cuneiform clay tablets. Cuneiform tablets were used in ancient Mesopotamia. Upon them, people of 3,000 to 5,000 years ago recorded information and history. These fragile tablets are often discovered in fragments and measure about the size of a deck of playing cards. Finding one is about as rare as finding a person who can understand the symbols of the ancient Mesopotamian language. Finkel has devoted his life's work to the study and preservation of these ancient texts.

Before and during World War II, the Middle East saw its share of occupations and armies. There were few laws or means to protect antiquities from leaving countries. Many members of the armed forces carried home historical relics. Some of the pieces were thousands of years old. These antiquities were passed down generationally and often wound up in the hands of grandchildren and great-grandchildren who did not know what they possessed, so for one of these tablets to surface is very rare. Cuneiform tablets are quite meaningful and historically valuable. They inform us about ancient times, allow historians to piece together the truth behind stories, and make sense of religious anecdotes. Each cuneiform is a metaphorical jigsaw puzzle helping to shape the overall picture of history.

Noah's ark is described in the Book of Genesis as the ship on which Noah gathered two of every creature on Earth before a great flood wiped the planet clean. Genesis goes on to describe the size of the ark. The ark was fifty cubits wide by thirty cubits tall by three hundred cubits long. A cubit is about the length of an arm. This was a large vessel. This size is specific, and our view and what we perceive as the reality of Noah's ark is that it was shaped a lot like a cruise ship.

In 2010, Dr. Finkel was sitting in his office at the British Museum when a young man, a descendant of a British World War II soldier, entered with a 4,000-year-old cuneiform. Each cuneiform has a story to tell. This one was different, and Dr. Finkel instantly knew it. Unbelievably, this cuneiform referred to an ancient flood and the building of a boat, the story of Noah. Dr. Finkel claimed in an interview that "this is one of the most important human documents ever to be discovered." It is important to consider the age of the cuneiform. Four thousand years predates the modern and edited versions of the Bible, and more significantly, it is from the same period as the tablets of *The Epic of Gilgamesh*. The closer any account is to an actual event, the more accurate the account is. The beauty of this cuneiform was that unlike the boat described in the ninth tablet of *The Epic of Gilgamesh*, this clay tablet gave the dimensions of the vessel. This probably was left out of the epic poem because that would be like stopping right in the middle of an action scene in a Batman movie to describe how the Batmobile's engine works. It would wreck the adventure. The cuneiform that the young man brought would challenge nearly all stories, renditions, and drawings of how Noah's craft looked. Noah's story was about to be rewritten.

Dr. Finkel is a scientist and a historian. In science, there are times when a scientific hypothesis is turned on its head. Sometimes data contradicts what is expected. And the best scientists can take a deep breath and accept when their initial instincts were proven to be incorrect. The Bible, however, is a religious text, and though it has been revised over millennia, essentially, major changes to the Bible are not taken lightly. If a discovery is to be made that changes a religious text that millions of people over thousands of years have based their spiritual foundation on, it is likely to raise more than just a few eyebrows.

The cuneiform's text indicated that Noah's ark looked different than thought before. It was circular, and according to the text, the boat was about two-hundred and twenty feet in diameter. Even more surprising was that the author of the cuneiform gave specific details about how the boat was built. Unlike the wooden boat that most modern renditions of the ark depict, the ark described on the clay tablet was made like a coracle. A coracle is a boat still used in remote Iraqi villages that looks like a rounded pot floating in the water. It is made with a frame of tightly wound grasses bound with rope. The entire boat is coated with bitumen, a thick tar-like substance that is created when petroleum is distilled. The bitumen keeps the boat from leaking.

In 1939, J. Abner Peddiwell published the book The Saber-tooth Curriculum. The story begins at a bar in Tijuana, Mexico, whose owner claims it is the world's longest bar. The simple fact of sitting at the world's longest bar is just the first in a string of examples used in the book to illustrate that we believe what we hear, see, and most importantly, are taught. The title itself is one more example from the book. From the title, Peddiwell argues, "How do we know what a saber tooth tiger looked like?" It is a valid point; we all have the image of the saber-tooth tiger in our minds, but we certainly cannot prove that our images are correct. There are no saber-tooth tigers in zoos, and many people have never seen the fossils; even with the fossils, scientists can only recreate so much. How do we have an image in our mind? Nearly everything people identify and imagine has been told to them. The book argues that we can be misguided and advocates for open-mindedness by reminding readers that new and contradictory information can come at any time.

Noah's ark was three hundred cubits by thirty cubits by fifty cubits. Or, was it? Dr. Finkel's discovery is an invaluable reminder about the importance of being openminded. What would have happened to the cuneiform if Finkel had dismissed it because of his prior knowledge the ark that is described in the book of Genesis? The description in the Bible contradicts the account on the cuneiform. Had Finkel not been openminded, he may have called the cuneiform a fraud.

Finkel's example teaches us to not be afraid of the facts; his assertion challenges what is written in the Bible. His intentions are not to alter people's spiritual beliefs. He is simply doing what scientists do. He is looking at the facts that are in front of him, and in this case a vessel is described that contradicts previous texts. Finkel received backlash when he first made his findings known to the public. Ironically, Finkel believes that the flood story was a Babylonian tale made up to scare people away from sinning. To be true to the cuneiform's description, even Finkel had to set aside his own beliefs. Regardless, the new findings challenge what we have been taught all along. The further time gets us away from a historical event, the more impact that the person writing down the history plays on what we understand as truth. The event Finkel's cuneiform describes is thousands of years old, translated through many languages, and revised by many human interpretations.

Other examples parallel the ark find. In December of 1901, after two and a half years of trying to control of the wing of their gliders, the Wright brothers found that Otto Lilienthal's mathematical calculations were incorrect. Up until that point, Lilienthal's data was universally considered to be the basis for any and all wing data necessary for flight. If the Wright brothers had not questioned the expert data of the time, they would have never achieved human flight.

Successful people know that there is a need to think unconventionally. They also realize that there is no need to reinvent the wheel, but there is always an open door to reinvent themselves. Successful people recognize when an improvement or new idea comes their way; they are not as quick as the naysayers to dismiss new ideas or information. Sometimes, like the ark, misconceptions weave themselves into religion and culture. Breakthroughs only come when people remain open-minded and ready for the truth.

## Conclusion

A MARATHON IS 26.2 miles long; a person does not just get up off the couch and run one. A heart surgeon does not just miraculously pick up a scalpel and begin a surgery. A kindergartener does not wake up from a nap and know calculus. Real change happens when years of training take place. This book was written with the intent to help you begin or enhance the process of looking at the world, history, and people through unconventional lenses. The events and circumstances in this book are just a small sliver of the different ways to understand how success is generated. Just like running, surgery, and mathematics, thinking unconventionally takes years—perhaps even a lifetime—of practice.

Growing up, I had an unconventional mother. She dealt with my undiagnosed hyperactivity by giving me a watercolor paintbrush to go between flowering fruit trees to paint blossoms. Going from tree to tree with pollen on the brush's fibers increased the rate of pollination, and in the fall, we had an abundance of fruit. This life experience is a metaphor for thinking unconventionally; insects can, of course, pollinate the world, but there are unconventional means to help them along. Today, it would be so easy to take a kid to the doctor, pop a few pills in his mouth, stick him in front of a videogame, or pay a sitter to watch him. From my earliest memories, I recall being taught unconventionally.

When I was twenty-three, I became a middle school technology teacher in West Virginia. I shared at the beginning of this book that I was faced with a new challenge: how to integrate the internet as a tool to be used in school. I overcame this challenge with the unconventional creativity I was taught as a child. It would have been easy to pay millions of dollars for a company to come in and wire a school, but our school did not have this type of capital. Instead, I used the opportunity to empower some of my twelve-year-old students. Though they were young, their motivation and clear understanding of a new generation of electronic networks created the first internet connections in the school's history.

Years later, I am now teaching 4th grade in Brockport, New York. When a child with cerebral palsy suddenly exposed his dream to become a cop, we formed a running team. Teaching self-esteem through running seems like a stretch for someone who already has physical challenges. Unconventional thinking brings on the mindset of let us find a way. In 2012, our 4th grade class made world news about a project in which we challenged the impossible. Our class released wine bottles into the Atlantic, only to conquer insurmountable odds when five of them washed up in Nova Scotia, the Azores, France, Portugal, and England. We live two hundred miles from an ocean, and we did not know anyone that had a seafaring boat. It took some original thinking to pursue the ideas generated after a student reported on a bottle washing ashore in Germany twenty-five years after it was launched. Our class worked together to find the unconventional means to get those forty-three original bottles in the Gulf Stream.

I am not Thomas Edison, and I will never have the genius of Albert Einstein. Most likely, I will never go into space, be canonized as a saint, or have a conversation with Paul McCartney. However, we all are on a life journey. Every single person that is walking this Earth has value. Patterns exist in our world, and those patterns have pushed all of us, without knowing it, into conformity. Conformity creates limits we often do not recognize, and it affects the level of success that each of us can achieve. For most of us, we cannot even begin to understand how vast our capabilities are. The fact is, we are entirely capable of greatness, creating new ideas, and discovering others. Just because there are five billion people on this planet does not mean that you cannot be the first person to carve a new path. In fact, new routes are created every day by people who have actively worked for years to create them. Years of practice, thoughtfulness, and discipline have led to amazing achievements. The arrows that point toward success are often found in the most unusual places. Search for the hidden arrows.

I shared that I teach nine- and ten-year-old children. There is a lot to learn from children. They often do not see the boundaries that adults do, and usually their ideas end up teaching me. Wait—I am a teacher, right? Aren't I the one who is supposed to have the answers and create the lessons? While it may seem counterintuitive, the answer is no. With as many attempts as I have made trying to define and redefine myself, my twenty-five years of teaching tell me precisely what I have heard in church many times: remember to listen to the children.

I thank you for considering my stories and words through this book. May you find joy and success in your life's journey. Dare to be and think unconventionally.

# Epilogue

When I was a boy, I collected dominoes. I saw a program on the television about a person who set a record by setting up and toppling tens of thousands of dominoes in a large gymnasium. I remember being fascinated by how that person spent weeks setting up the dominoes only to see them all topple in just a few minutes. Each domino had a role to push over the next one in line. Life is a set of toppling dominoes. For all the dominoes to fall, the first one has to be pushed.

Mrs. Pirrello was my first-grade teacher and Mr. Karg was my fifth-grade teacher. They are the reason I became a teacher. They were the dominoes that caused my domino to fall. Ironically, nobody will never fully know which domino they pushed over. We are not readers of minds and will never know the full impact we have had on others. We have contrasting memories of Mrs. Pirrello and Mr. Karg. I have a few explicit memories of Mrs. Pirrello, but I have hundreds of detailed memories of Mr. Karg. What I know is I looked forward to going to school every day I was in their classes. The common denominator between these two very different educators is that they played significant roles in developing my positive self-concept and created a world where I felt successful. Mrs. Pirrello was soft spoken, creative and patient. Mr. Karg was loud, full of energy and unpredictable. My guess is both were authentic people, meaning that their actions inside and outside of school were consistent. The common thread between Mrs. Pirrello and Mr. Karg is that they saw the differences between each student and were able to reach students based on their gifts and needs. They reached me, and I am so very thankful for this.

After I became the New York State Teacher of the Year, I began traveling to schools. I asked to teach and present on the importance of kindness, tolerance, empathy, and literacy. In honor of Mrs. Pirrello and Mr. Karg, the last school I visited was Brooks Hill School in Fairport, New York. This is where I went to school. Mrs. Pirrello joined me in spirit, and Mr. Karg joined me in person. It was the first time since I was twelve that I had revisited. I now have gray whiskers and am no longer that high energy kid that attended the school forty years prior.

My memories had built Brooks Hill School to be a magical kingdom. When I returned, a strange reality hit me. Brooks Hill looks a lot like the school I teach in; not structurally, but the actions of the students and teachers mirror my school. After the day at my childhood school, I realized that my first domino had nothing to do with where I grew up. It had everything to do with the relationships I had with my teachers. Mr. Karg is now a 43-year veteran educator. We went back to room 316, the classroom we shared in 1982-83. On that day he proved to me that I was not just his former student but instead his friend for life. That is unconventional. It seemed like a simple revelation, but it has such significant meaning. It validated why I teach and why I am the person I have become.

## About the Author

Born and raised in Fairport, New York, Christopher Albrecht fell in love with school at an early age. For as long as he can remember, school has been a magical place with endless possibilities full of teachers and coaches he admired. As a first-generation American son of his German father, Albrecht grew up hearing many stories about history, while being influenced by his highly artistic mother. The combination of his homelife and schooling developed his mindset and the foundation for this book.

Christopher Albrecht is the 2018 New York State Teacher of the Year and is a 2019 inductee into the National Teachers Hall of Fame in Emporia, Kansas. He has authored two TEDx Talks: "Dust and Sneakers, Crawling and Running" and "Giftedness for All."

Albrecht began his career in 1995 in New Martinsville, West

Virginia teaching middle school technology in the morning and kindergarten in the afternoon. His first teaching experiences coincided with rapid changes in technology and the innovation of the internet. His pioneering work in technology earned him the 1996 Sallie Mae National First-Class Teacher Award.

In 1998, Albrecht returned to upstate New York. He currently teaches 4th grade at the Fred W. Hill School in Brockport. He is an adjunct professor in the Department of Education at the SUNY College at Brockport.

Albrecht holds a Bachelor of Science degree in Elementary Education from St. Bonaventure University and a master's degree in Elementary Education from Clarion University. A lifelong learner at heart, he recently became a National Geographic Certified Educator.

In 2018, Albrecht was inducted into the St. Bonaventure University Wall of Distinguished Educators and is currently a member of the Fairport High School Alumni Wall of Fame, where he graduated in 1990.

Christopher and his wife, Jennifer, have raised three children (Autumn, Cory, and Aaron) and live in Brockport, New York, the town in which he teaches. He has a passion for backcountry hiking, geology, baseball, and National Parks.

www.ingramcontent.com/pod-product-compliance
Lightning Source LLC
Chambersburg PA
CBHW021313020526
44118CB00047B/588